D0828454

The Politics of Domesticity

THE
POLITICS
OF
DOMESTICITY

Women, Evangelism, and Temperance
in Nineteenth-Century America

by

BARBARA LESLIE EPSTEIN

Wesleyan University Press
Middletown, Connecticut

Library of Congress Cataloging in Publication Data

Epstein, Barbara Leslie, 1944–
The politics of domesticity.

Bibliography: p.
Includes index.
1. Feminism—United States—History—19th century.
2. Temperance—History—19th century.   3. Women in
Christianity—United States—History—19th century.
4. Revivals—United States—History—19th century.
5. United States—Church history.   I.   Title.
HQ1423.E67   305.4′2   80-16671
ISBN 0-8195-5050-7

Distributed by Columbia University Press
136 South Broadway, Irvington, NY 10533

Manufactured in the United States of America
First edition

To my mother,
Marion Easton

Contents

Acknowledgments

THIS BOOK would never have been written without the help of friends and colleagues. My greatest debt is to David Plotke, who, as friend, editor, and intellectual critic, helped me to write a much better book than I would otherwise have done. His perceptive criticisms and suggestions enabled me to frame the project as a whole and draw out its strenghts, and with encouragement and support he prevailed upon me to do the best job that I could. Lawrence Levine supervised my dissertation, suggested that I turn it into a book, and gave me direction in doing so. Harry Levine, who is writing a book on the temperance movement, gave me great help in my study of the Woman's Crusade and the WCTU. With rare generosity, he introduced me to much of the literature that I used, pointed out many specific quotes, and helped me to formulate my approach to the subject. Many of the issues that I discuss in the chapters on these topics came from my discussions with Harry or from his comments on drafts. Ellen Du Bois read the final drafts of the manuscript and criticized them with care and incisiveness. Her knowledge of the history of feminism, women's history, and nineteenth-century America strengthened the book greatly. Claudia Carr helped me to place my work in a broad analytical framework, and in innumerable discussions she endeavored to keep my mind sharp. Her friendship helped to counter the isolation of research and writing.

The book benefited from criticisms and suggestions made by Ruth Bloch, Nancy Chodorow, Kenneth Kann, Eben Moglen, Lillian Rubin, Kathryn Sklar, Lawrence Veysey, Alan Wolfe, and Alfred Young. Marsha Millman, Helene Moglen, Norma Wikler, and Carol Wolman gave me not only helpful criticisms but much appreciated support in completing the project. Nancy Cott pointed me to important archival sources, and Rosalita Leonard of the Woman's Christian Temperance Union guided me through the holdings of the WCTU library. Mary Ryan and Norma Wikler gave the book its name.

I was supported during parts of this project by Faculty Research Funds granted by the University of California, Santa Cruz.

The Politics of Domesticity

Introduction

THIS BOOK traces the emergence of a popular women's consciouness of difference from, and antagonism to, men, developing through four phases of
women's religious activity, from the mid eighteenth century through the late
nineteenth century. The first phase was the Great Awakening of 1740–44
and the revivals that immediately followed it. Women participated in these
revivals, evidently in numbers equal to men, but no particular female consciousness, and for that matter no particular female role, seems to have
emerged. The second phase was the female evangelism of the Second Great
Awakening of 1797–1840. Here women played an instrumental role in
fostering revivals, and women's piety took on a militancy that was directed
especially against irreligious or insufficiently pious men. In the latter half of
the nineteenth century, women's religious activity began to incorporate
certain secular concerns. (Among men such secularization had been
apparent since at least the turn of the nineteenth century.) Yet these female
reform movements did not become independent, continuing, often, to be
based in the church.

The Woman's Crusade of 1873–75, the third phase of this history of
women's religious activity, was a movement of midwestern Protestant
women endeavoring to close down the saloons that they saw as threatening
the religious and moral standards with which they identified. Here, for the
first time, groups of women pitted themselves against what they saw as institutions of male culture. The Woman's Christian Temperance Union
emerged out of the demise of the Woman's Crusade. The women's
temperance movement of the last two decades of the nineteenth century,
which the WCTU encompassed, constitutes the fourth phase of this history.
Within the WCTU the tradition of female evangelism was transformed into
social morality defined in religious terms, centered around the defense of the
family and of "home values." The WCTU developed a protofeminist politics
in which women's interests, as the WCTU defined them, took primacy and in

which the vote was seen as a necessary weapon for the defense of the institutions and values that the WCTU upheld.

This development of women's religious activity and the emergence from it of what women came to regard as a particularly "female" set of concerns and values paralleled and I believe was shaped by another development: the reorganization of relations between men and women within the amorphous constellations of social groups (the "middling classes") that emerged with the nineteenth-century growth of the market and beginnings of industrialization. When they moved to the towns and cities, separating themselves from their rural origins and the family farm, women lost the direct involvement that they had once had in economic production and came to be confined to the tasks of child care, housework, and the creation of the home as a refuge for men. Some women helped to sustain businesses that were run from the home. But efficiency dictated workplaces outside the home, and the growth of towns brought pressures to locate them in business districts. Young women might work for a time before marrying, and poor women routinely contributed to the family income by taking in sewing or laundry, but for women of the "middling classes" marriage meant domesticity, which meant economic dependence on a man. The confinement of women to a distinct sphere of activities provided a basis for a distinct set of values; their heightened dependence on men brought a greater subordination to them. In a milieu in which independence was highly valued, resentment often lay close to the surface.

Domesticity and Protestant evangelism were the two bases for a set of values articulated with growing clarity, through the nineteenth century, by a large number of American women. These women often thought of themselves as representing womanhood generally, or at least American womanhood. It is important to remember that their experience and their values were particular to them, not, as they often thought, universal. The history traced in this book is that of a group of white, American-born women of New England stock and, for the most part, English and Puritan ancestry. The perspective of these women was shaped by their location in a particular class and a particular region of the country and by their immersion in the Protestant tradition.

The first of the phases of religious activity under study took place before the family was reorganized into a domestic unit and before class differences became a salient characteristic of the New England countryside. The revivals of the Great Awakening took place largely in socially homogeneous villages of farming families. The next three phases of activity took place in the commercial, industrializing towns of New England and the Midwest. Heightened market activity and industry provided the basis for a swelling of nonfarming occupations. The women who participated in these latter phases of religious activity were likely to be the wives or daughters of skilled artisans, shopkeepers, traders, professionals. Such people were aware of the social difference between themselves and those who remained in the countryside, and between themselves and the families of less skilled workers. In the 1830s it is possible to see the beginnings of an American working class in the towns of New England; by the late nineteenth century this class had become a significant social force and was made up in large part of immigrants whose traditions, even when Protestant, were quite different from those of the more established Anglo-Americans. In the late nineteenth century class conflict as well as conflict between the sexes helped to shape the perspective of middle-class women.

Both the evangelical and temperance movements were important in forming what might loosely be called the nineteenth-century middle class, as well as in shaping the outlook of groups of workers, especially skilled workers. In the nineteenth century, the term *middling classes* was often used in place of the more modern *middle class* and more accurately suggested a disparate grouping rather than a homogeneous whole. This grouping included professionals, shopkeepers and other tradespeople, independent artisans, possibly skilled workers, urban people who were neither wealthy nor desperately poor and who hoped to find some avenue of upward mobility in the expanding market of nineteenth-century America. The middling classes were as much a cultural and ideological as an economic category, and evangelism and temperance were two of the central issues around which struggles over culture and ideology were conducted. Both movements raised the issues of individual morality and self-control that seemed to many to be avenues to upward mobility and, especially in the latter part of the century, to be means of maintaining boundaries against, and control over, the new immigrant working class. Along with piety and sobriety, domesticity was an issue in the formation of the nineteenth-century middling classes: domesticity was for the comfortable and respectable to practice, and for the poor to aspire to. A man's ability to support his wife at home was a measure of success; inability to do so was a cause of shame. Domesticity raised very different issues for women than it did for men; it brought a greater measure of material comfort and entailed an enhancement of women's moral influence, but it also meant confinement to what came to seem a narrow set of roles. Both gender and class were redefined in ways that have had far-reaching significance; female social action was one of the forces contributing to this redefinition. In particular, women's evangelism and women's temperance shaped, and were shaped by, the issues of gender and class.

Nineteenth-century America saw the emergence not only of the popular women's culture that these movements gave expression to but also of feminism. The central goal of feminism was and is the attainment of equality between men and women; nineteenth-century feminism took the question of female equality in the public arena as its main issue, recognizing—but for the time largely putting aside—the question of the inequality of the sexes within the family. The emerging popular women's culture at times over-lapped quite significantly with feminism. Both women's religious activity and women's temperance were motivated to a large degree by women's anger over their subordinate status, and for much of the late nineteenth century the women's temperance movement supported the feminist goals of woman suffrage and of woman's equality in the public arena. For feminism, women's equality was the central goal; women's evangelism and women's temperance took as their central goal the moral reformation of American life, a goal that by the last quarter of the century had focussed, within the temperance movement, upon the slogan of "Home Protection." During the last quarter of the century feminism and popular women's culture converged in that many women believed that female suffrage and female equality in public life generally would be the means by which moral reformation and defense of the home would be achieved. But where the interests of women and the defense of the nineteenth-century middle-class family (and the morality that was associated with it) diverged, the women's temperance movement chose the latter.

The analysis in this book of the development of a women's conscious-ness in nineteenth-century America is framed by three distinct concepts: sexual difference, sexual antagonism, and feminism. In every known society social distinctions have been drawn between the sexes, centered around women's special responsibility for child care and justified by (though not made necessary by) women's ability to bear and nurse children. Social difference between men and women may or may not produce antagonism, and it may produce various degrees of antagonism, depending upon the nature of the social relations within which that social difference, or division of labor, is embedded. In colonial New England there was a clear distinction between the familial and social functions and standing of men and women. Though male dominance and female subordination were clearly present, no pattern of female antagonism toward men in accounts of religious activity and experience has been found. In nineteenth-century America, the division of labor between men and women was redefined, and the distance between the sexes widened, by domesticity. The religious experience of middle-class women in the first half of the century and, to an even greater extent, the women's temperance movement in the latter part of the century suggest an increasingly explicit antagonism to men, producing an ideology that based its case for women on a universal morality rather than on a feminist demand for female equality.

Sexual difference, the division of labor in the family and the delineation of roles and rights in society generally, does not always produce expressions of sexual antagonism. What was it about the relations between men and women in the towns of the nineteenth-century Northeast that led women to create a culture in which sexual difference became intertwined with questions of morality, and in which what were seen as masculine and feminine principles were placed in combat? How were the concepts of feminity and of relations between men and women that emerged within this culture affected by the class conflicts and ethnic hostilities of the time? The importance of these questions reaches into the present. Nineteenth-century popular women's culture, mediated through turn-of-the-century feminism, continues to have an impact upon American feminism, especially on the formulation of a feminist morality and the articulation of feminist attitudes toward sex and class.

The evangelical movement of the early nineteenth century and the temperance movement of the post–Civil War years were of course not the only movements of this period in which women of the northern United States participated. For much of the nineteenth century, movements for reform proliferated in and around New England, and from at least the 1830s on, women played a major role in many of them. Of these movements it is the most radical that have been most closely studied. For the subsequent history of American women, the abolitionist and the women's rights movements had a particular significance: the abolitionist movement because, in pointing to the oppression of the slave, it suggested the analogous problem of the oppression of women; and the women's rights movement because it raised the questions that would increasingly concern American women.

While these movements pointed to central issues, in their own time they remained minority tendencies. For a study of popular consciousness it is necessary to look at movements that were closer to the outlook of the majority. For women of the New England and midwestern middle class in the nineteenth century, these were the evangelical and temperance movements, based in the church, committed to the defense of religion and a conservative morality. In the context of Christian conservatism, in large part within these movements, these women gained the ability to understand the world in new terms, from a standpoint that was centered in women's experience and critical of society as it was. Religious revivals gave many women a relatively legitimate ground on which to meet with other women and an opportunity to voice their concerns and to begin to define their own values. Within the women's temperance movement of the last quarter of the century the vaguely defined, woman-oriented moral conservatism of the religious movement crystallized into a clearer political and social stance that combined a moral conservatism with some feminist demands.

This book examines two major periods of religious revivals in New England's history: the Great Awakening of 1740–44 and the years immediately following it, and the revivals of the first four decades of the nineteenth century. It compares women's and men's experiences in the revivals of these two periods and compares the patterns of experience in the two periods with each other. The account is drawn mainly from personal narratives of religious conversions, some of them preserved in church records, others published in evangelical journals. For the eighteenth century, two Massachusetts collections of conversion accounts, one from Sturbridge and the other from Chebacco (including, in all, the statements of eighty-three converts), are the primary sources, supplemented by religious diaries, descriptions of conversions and revivals in letters, and ministers' accounts of revivals over which they presided and conversions that they witnessed. For the nineteenth-century revivals, the main source is the evangelical press of the period, especially the *Connecticut Evangelical Magazine and Religious*

Intelligencer, which was published throughout the first half of the century (from 1800 through 1807 as the *Connecticut Evangelical Magazine,* from 1808 into 1816 as the *Connecticut Evangelical Magazine and Religious Intelligencer,* and thereafter as the *Religious Intelligencer*), and which regularly included letters from converts describing their own conversions. Additional sources are nineteenth-century letters including descriptions of revivals and conversions, accounts written by ministers and other observers. Forty-six reasonably detailed accounts of nineteenth-century conversions have been located, as have a large number of less detailed accounts.

Primary materials for the study of the late-nineteenth-century women's temperance crusade and union are considerably more accessible, though hardly more explored. A large number of participants in the Woman's Crusade wrote and published accounts of it, and the discussion of the crusade relies primarily on these accounts and to some extent on histories written by nonparticipants, most of whom were themselves advocates of temperance. The account of the WCTU relies primarily on the literature of the organization itself: the writings of Frances Willard, its president throughout the period in question; other literature published by the WCTU; the *Union Signal,* the organ of the WCTU; and the minutes of national conventions through the last two decades of the century. This provides, of course, only an account of the workings and outlook of the national organization; a more detailed study of the WCTU in this period would require a study of state conventions and publications.

A great deal of work has already been done on the history of American women in the nineteenth century, especially the history of middle-class New England women.[1] The women's rights movement, the family relations and personal lives of middle-class women, and the culture that these women constructed have all been explored fairly thoroughly. The historical interpretation on which this book rests—that female domesticity was linked to the destruction of an agrarian economy and the development of commercial and industrial capitalism and the town life that accompanied it—is widely accepted. It is also widely agreed that middle-class women of this time constructed their own social networks and a set of shared values and that this culture was created by rather than imposed upon women, though its limits were set by women's domesticity and dependence upon family relations and, more generally, by women's subordinate position within a male-dominant society.

What is potentially controversial about this book is its argument that this female culture was shaped by conflict between women and men, conflict that was often denied by women but was rooted in the structure of their relations with men and exacerbated by a society that devalued the dependent roles into which women were forced. Conflict between women and men could not be entirely suppressed even though the position of women was too weak for any but a minority to be willing to openly challenge male dominance. This muted conflict had an ongoing and unavoidable impact on women's actions and on their understanding of themselves and their world.

One book that does place middle-class female culture clearly in the context of sexual antagonism is Ann Douglas's *Feminization of American Culture,* a study of the alliance between Unitarian and Universalist ministers and a number of influential middle-class women and the impact of this alliance on middle-class popular culture in the latter part of the nineteenth century.[2] Douglas believes that the women whom she studies, many of them writers or active in reform movements, constituted a relatively coherent group, speaking for or at least representing the views of middle-class women more generally; she sees these women as having had, through their ties with and influence over ministers, a significant role in the liberalization of New England theology. Douglas suggests that, in combatting the austere and rigorous Puritanism of New England tradition, these women were combatting the authority and rule of the fathers; she argues that the weakening of this theology, and its replacement by a sentimental, reform-oriented religiosity, represented a female victory.

I endorse Douglas's view that the familial life of the nineteenth-century middle class was framed by conflict between the sexes, and also her understanding of middle-class women's culture as having been shaped by and used as a weapon in that conflict. But I do not see these women as a coherent group or as uniquely representative of American middle-class women. The evangelical women in this study, who were also part of that broad nineteenth-century social spectrum that can be called the middle class, identified themselves with the cause of Protestant orthodoxy rather than liberalism and turned that orthodoxy against men, whom they saw as trying to escape from genuine piety under the guise of a watered-down theology. These women also allied themselves with ministers, in this case the ministers who identified themselves as Calvinists rather than Universalists or Unitarians. The "orthodoxy" of the nineteenth century was of course dif-

ferent from the Calvinism of the previous two centuries, although it iden-
tififed itself with that tradition; nevertheless, the women in this study saw
themselves as defending old values, values that seemed threatened by the
new social order.

Douglas is right, I think, in suggesting that conflicts rooted in the
nineteenth-century middle class were played out in the arena of culture,
especially religion, and that on this terrain middle-class women were able to
exert some influence. But I think she sees the stance of middle-class women
as more coherent and less ambivalent than it was, and I think she exag-
gerates the power of these women. Unlike Douglas, I see nineteenth-century
female culture as internally conflicted and contradictory, confined by the
limits established by the well-entrenched power of men, defensive in relation
to male dominance and unable to challenge it in fundamental ways. Popular
women's culture in nineteenth-century America, in my view, expressed a
complex amalgam of reactions to male power: protest, resentment, disapproval, fear, accommodation. The criticisms that religious and temperance
women made of male behavior were accepted by the middling classes as a
whole only when those criticisms coincide with men's own self-criticisms,
their own perceptions of the changes they needed to make in their own self-
interest. Thus, even though temperance was, by the late nineteenth century,
strongly identified with women, the gradual acceptance of temperance cannot be seen as simply the result of women's effective exercise of their
influence. Sobriety was seen by an increasing number of men as necessary to
success in the nineteenth-century scramble for upward mobility.

All of this is to say that popular women's culture should be distinguished from feminism, though by the late nineteenth century it was
influenced by feminism and overlapped with it to a considerable degree. The
clearest, most consistent challenge directed at male power in nineteenth-
century America came not from the popular women's culture that Douglas
and I examine but from the feminist movement. Nineteenth-century middle-
class women were confined and constrained by domesticity and by the extreme
imbalance of power between the sexes that domesticity created. Within that
situation women did what they could; neither a reconstruction of relations
between the sexes nor a reconstruction of culture that would genuinely
empower women and limit male dominance lay within their abilities. These
women's accomplishments and the limitations of those accomplishments
helped to shape women's lives in the nineteenth century and since.

Religious Conversions in the Eighteenth Century: The Shared Experience of Men and Women

THE GREAT AWAKENING was the first great mass movement in American history. Especially in New England, where it began and where it was centered throughout its course, the Awakening amounted to a social earthquake, touching virtually every community, involving men and women of all ages and all social levels. During the revivals of the Awakening, religious conversion ceased to be a primarily individual experience; religion became infectious, and conversion took on the character of a collective experience. The Great Awakening derived its power from this collectivization of religious feeling. Traditionally, religion had been defined by the elite and accepted relatively passively by the people; the Awakening threatened to reverse this process, giving ordinary people the confidence to propagate actively religion as they understood it and at times even to press their understandings of piety upon their ministers.

The Great Awakening shook long-established habits of deference and passivity, encouraging ordinary people to speak for themselves in a new way. For this reason, it has a special place in the popular history of New England. And because women participated in the revivals of the Awakening and those that followed it in at least as large numbers as men, it also has a special place in the history of women in this period. The lives of eighteenth-century women were usually even more constricted than those of their men; the opportunities that revivals brought for social interaction and for self-expression must have seemed particularly emancipating to women who participated in them. It is difficult enough to find statements by eighteenth-century men of their concerns; it is even harder to find records of moments in which women of this time asserted themselves in this way. The conversion accounts of the revivals of the mid-eighteenth century record moments when ordinary men and women spoke of some of their deepest concerns and indicated the world view that shaped their perceptions.

The Awakening can be said to have begun in Jonathan Edwards's congregation in Northampton, Massachusetts, where a revival took place in 1735 that shook the community and spread to surrounding towns as well. For the next several years this experience was not repeated, but in 1740 when George Whitefield, an English Presbyterian, toured the colonies, his sermons set off revivals wherever he went. After he left the colonies, the revivals continued, spreading most rapidly in New England, where itinerant preachers went from town to town, speaking from the pulpits of sympathetic ministers and in private homes or in the open air where local ministers opposed the Awakening.

From 1741 to 1744 revivals also spread spontaneously: even in towns where the clergy was unsympathetic, each conversion inspired more conversions, and revivals spread from town to town as converts wrote or visited friends and relatives. Ministerial opposition, which tended to increase as the enthusiasm of the Awakening mounted, did little to discourage the revivals. Widespread popular concern with the religious matters was not new in New England, but during the Great Awakening large numbers of people assumed unprecedented responsibility for the stances of their churches. Ministers who were uncertain of their attitude toward the Awakening might be visited by delegations from their congregations, urging their support; ministers who were hostile might find sections of their congregations breaking off to form new churches.[1]

Edwards and Whitefield had stressed the traditional themes of human degeneracy and the need to seek God's mercy if one hoped to escape hell. This message touched a chord, especially in New England, where the relative religious coolness that had prevailed in the decades before the Awakening stood in greatest contrast to the religiosity of the early generations. This decline in religiosity was undoubtedly related to the social and demographic changes that New England had undergone since the late seventeenth century. In the first decades of settlement, the profound religiosity of a self-selected group of immigrants had been protected by the relative stability of a largely agricultural and highly localized society. With few distractions from religion, the church maintained its hegemony with relative ease. By the first decades of the eighteenth century, the growth of commercial farming and the increase in land speculation was contributing to behavior that could bring people into conflict either with church authorities or with their own religiously informed consciences. Even in areas where trade was as yet relatively undeveloped, population growth generated conflicts within communities that undermined social unity and often weakened the authority of the church.[2]

Eighteenth-century New Englanders were more likely to drift away from the church than clearly to reject orthodox religion, partly because their religious heritage was too strong to be put aside easily and partly because as yet there was no alternate ideology with which it could be replaced. New behavior that continues to be judged according to old standards can only be found wanting: the process of drift was accompanied by profound guilt, which, as it accumulated over the decades, made possible an explosion of the proportions of the Great Awakening. By the late eighteenth century a secular liberalism would emerge that would allow those New Englanders who came into contact with it to see their own declining religious fervor and their increasingly individualistic behavior in a more positive light. But at the time of the Great Awakening, only the faintest hints of such rationalistic secularism had reached New England. People who found themselves drifting away from the church and avidly pursuing their economic self-interest could understand their behavior only as moral defection.

The revivals of the Great Awakening, and of the decade that followed it, emerged out of the widespread desire for the reaffirmation of religious fervor and orthodox doctrine that such guilt engendered. In this sense the Awakening represented traditionalism, an attempt to re-create a "golden age" of piety. This was the side of the Awakening that its defenders, ministers such as Jonathan Edwards, stressed in seeking the support of wavering or hostile clergy. Where Edwards saw the piety of the Awakening, its critics saw its other side: in the name of tradional piety, promoters of the Awakening were allowing ordinary people to challenge the authority of their ministers. Itinerants and other revivalists, in criticizing ministers for lack of zeal and in appealing to the people for support, were in effect undermining traditional patterns of deference. By extension the Awakening could be seen as posing a threat not only to established religion but to a social order that was based on obedience to superiors.[3]

The Great Awakening, in fact, was both of these things: it attempted to turn the church back toward traditional piety, and it expressed and reinforced popular discontent with established authorities. It was this combination that allowed the Awakening to become as popular, and as socially explosive, as it was. Because the Awakening was so deeply rooted in popular consciousness, it allows us a rare opportunity to examine the outlook and the concerns of colonial New Englanders whose views would ordinarily be quickly forgotten. During the revivals of the Great Awakening and those of the following years, some churches recorded and preserved the conversion experiences of ordinary men and women; their accounts sum up extensive emotional experience and point to central concerns among the converts.

The experiences of these men and women were remarkably similar, revealing a range of concerns that do not sort themselves easily according to the sex of the convert. Men and women followed the same patterns of conversion, spoke of the same kinds of sins, and described their experiences in similar language. If there is no signature at the bottom of a particular conversion narrative, there is often no way of knowing whether the author was male or female. On close examination of these narratives, it becomes apparent that there are some subtle differences. But the most important lesson to be drawn from a reading of these narratives is that these men and women thought and worried about very much the same things and that they resolved their problems in similar ways. Particularly when set against the conversion experiences of nineteenth-century New Englanders, which would vary so greatly by sex, the similarity of men's and women's accounts in the eighteenth century is striking.

Calvinism and Conversion

Both eighteenth- and nineteenth-century conversions were Calvinist, and for the most part they followed the prescribed Calvinist pattern. Often, upon learning of the death of an unsaved person, hearing a particularly affecting sermon, or seeing others convert, a man or woman would undergo *convictions*: a sharp awareness of sin, fears of hell, and a strong desire to be saved. Two kinds of sins would come to mind: after considering actual sins or "sins of the world"—particular misdeeds that now provoked guilt and fear of damnation—usually the person would move to a concern with original sin or "sins of the heart"—irrepressible evil thoughts, a sense of an innate sinfulness that could not be obliterated by any action regardless of its worth. Ultimately the person would find relief from this despair, perhaps being convinced by a dream or a recurring biblical phrase that Christ had interceded and God had granted salvation. Depression would be followed by elation, a sense of having been united with God and having conquered hell.

Within this pattern variations were possible. Convictions might vary widely in duration and emotional intensity: some people considered suicide while others passed through the experience with relative ease; some suffered for months or even years, while others found relief after a few days or even less. The emphasis might be on either actual or original sin: some people left out actual sins altogether, not being able to recall any, while others spoke only of their actual sins, mentioning original sin not at all or only under the prodding of a preacher or religious friend or relative. And salvation itself could come in various ways. A few people, especially in the eighteenth century, had visions of God. Ministers generally discouraged this; according to Calvinist belief God had revealed himself directly only in biblical times, so such visions were usually considered the products of an overheated imagination or even of the devil's intervention. More conventionally, a sudden and overpowering love for God, an acceptance of his omnipotence, or simply release from the torment of convictions was taken as evidence of salvation. The many thousands of New Englanders who converted in the eighteenth and nineteenth centuries followed this Calvinist pattern because it was traditional and expected: they had been taught that a true conversion must take this form, and ministers and those already converted helped to keep prospective converts on this path.

Written accounts of eighteenth-century conversions were usually unpolished. Many eighteenth-century converts wrote with difficulty, and even those who dictated their accounts to a minister seem to have spoken with some hesitation, their narrative often being strictly chronological, with special emphasis on the accepted turning points of conversion: awakening, convictions, salvation. These people were anxious to demonstrate to the minister and to the congregation of the church to which they were making application that their conversions were sound and orthodox, and they went carefully through each stage of conversion, often quoting from the Bible or from sermons they had heard to demonstrate the orthodoxy of the experience.

From these accounts, religious awakening often followed a particularly affecting sermon; converts spoke of having been shaken by a phrase that seemed particularly appropriate to themselves. Esther Williams of Chebacco, for instance, was awakened by a sermon directed toward young people, "whereby," she said, "I was bro't to see I was guilty of setting Lyes to make Sport, breaking the Sabbath, and disobedience to parents."[4] Others began to think seriously about religion upon seeing others convert. Daniel Low recounted, "I was never under any convictions before the fifth Sabbath after Thanksgiving last year; there hearing some of my mates . . . in the meeting house bro't me under concern. Some of my actual sins were bro't to my mind."[5]

Themes of Conversion: The Fear of Growing Worldliness

Usually concern first centered on particular sins; among these, indifference to religion, disobedience to parents, and frivolous or "worldly" behavior were the most commonly mentioned. Moses Holbrook of Sturbridge wrote,

> I have rebelled against God and my parence in living in all most all manner of Sin in Sabbath breaking and Company keeping and disabaying my parence good Counsel and instructions that they gave me in telling me it was my duty to Seeke to God in prayer. . . . I being young thought that it was time Enough.[6]

Many converts focused their attention upon misdeeds that earlier had not seemed so wicked but that now loomed large; performance of religious duties without real feeling was salient among such sins. The minister in Halifax, Massachusetts, wrote of a woman in his congregation who

> trembled under a sense of guilt, particularly because of the sin of Unbelief and the Hardness of her Heart; she said . . . that she was the Hypocrite. On the Sabbath, while in church this tho't pierced her soul, "How in that place she had dishonoured Christ by receiving the Sacrament unworthily." She was affected to such a degree as to overcome her bodily strength.[7]

Some showed similar concern over misbehavior toward others that had not been evident to any but themselves. Nathan Cole, a farmer who lived outside Hartford, Connecticut, and who had been initially awakened by a sermon preached by George Whitefield in that town, wrote of the self-examination that ensued:

> I carried such a weight of Sin in my breast or mind, that it seemed to me as if I should sink into the ground every step. . . . I thought I must go to my Honoured

Mother and Father to ask their forgiveness for everything I had done amiss toward them in all my life. . . . [I] asked them to forgive everything they had against me concerning my disobedience or whatever else it might be. They said they had not anything against me.[8]

As religious concerns grew, people were encouraged to shift the focus of that concern from particular misdeeds to the state of their souls generally, to the original sin that they had inherited from Adam and Eve. According to Calvinist theory, the initial disobedience that Adam and Eve had shown to God had been and would always be passed on from one generation to the next. Thus, every child was condemned to be born with a sinful and rebellious heart, one that must be changed in order to attain any hope of salvation. God and Christ, according to this view, were already to receive sinners and to offer them mercy, but sinners must first open themselves to divine love. In order to prepare for salvation, each person was instructed to consider and repent not only concrete misdeeds, actual sins, but also innate or original sin and to consider the damnation such sin deserved.

The degree of emphasis placed upon each of these categories, actual and original sins, varied. Some felt sharp anguish over specific misdeeds, while others passed quickly to consideration of their original sin. Hannah Bear was discouraged from prayer because of the enormity of her actual sins; for any one of them, she wrote, she justly could be sent to hell.[9] But those who passed quickly over their actual sins did not thereby gain confidence, for the original sin upon which they dwelt was greater than any actual sin could be. Elizabeth Perkins wrote, "I was bro't to see my actual sins which called for vengeance; after this, I was brought to see the sins of my nature, that I was wholly sinner from the Birth. I see I can't live without sinning against God and this is my greatest Burden. I long to be perfectly holy."[10] Other converts resisted seeing themselves in this way, arguing that they had done nothing to deserve damnation. In Jonathan Edwards's congregation in Northampton, Massachusetts, one young woman objected that it was unfair to be sent to hell for someone else's sin. She "entertained an opinion that she was not guilty of Adam's sin nor in any way connected with it, because she was not active in it."[11] Esther Williams recounted: "At first I could not see it was just to damn me for the Sin of my first parents which was committed thousands of years before I was born."[12]

For such people and for some others as well the onset of conversion was likely to be accompanied by anger at God: for condemning them for a sin they had not committed or simply for condemning them, even if such punishment was deserved, while he saved others. Sarah Kinsman wrote, "The first I was bro't under concern was by seeing those that had received comfort here rejoicing in Christ and praising God. . . . I could not bear it to think of their going to heaven and being left myself to go to hell."[13] Sarah Butler wrote, "I thought hard of God that he should take some that I thought were worse than I was." For these people a desire for salvation was at war with stubborn opposition to God and religion. Sarah Butler continued, "It seemed as if my heart had been barred or bolted against Christ and was not willing he should come into my heart."[14] The minister of the church in Middleborough, Massachusetts, wrote that many of those under conviction in his congregation "now complain they can't believe, find their hearts full of enmity to God, to Christ, to his holiness, his word, and Saints. Scores, this day, have told me of their Hatred of me above anyone."[15]

Such a sense of alienation from God and Christ, and from religion itself, was likely to result in great despair. Nathan Cole wrote of this stage of his conversion:

It pleased God to bring on my conviction more and more, and I was loaded with the guilt of sin, I saw I was undone for ever: I carried such a weight of Sin in my mind and breast, that it seemed to me as if I should sink into the ground every step. . . . I tried every way I could think to myself but every way failed. . . . Hell fire was almost always on my mind: and I have hundreds of times put my fingers into my pipe when I have been smoking to feel how fire felt: and to see how my Body could bear to Lie in Hell fire for ever and ever.[16]

Nathan Cole, like many others, expressed the terror of the conversion experience through metaphors of personal destruction; he was tormented by the thought of his physical vulnerability to the fires of hell. Sarah Kinsman became concerned about the state of her soul when her husband asked her "how she could bear to sleep over hell,"[17] and in Halifax, Massachusetts, a young girl while at play "fell down in great Distress," and reported that it seemed as if Hell lay before her, that she was ready to fall into it."[18] Isaac Proctor recounted that he was awakened by hearing a sermon in which the unawakened sinner was likened to a man sleeping next to a swarm of vipers that might sting him at any moment: this, he said, he saw to be his own case.[19]

Repeatedly, these converts expressed their fears of the natural world, their sense of their own frailty and mortality. Storms, earthquakes, illness, childbirth, the deaths of relatives and friends—all of these formed the background of religious awakening. Converts in both Chebacco and Sturbridge spoke of having been briefly awakened by the earthquake of 1755, five to ten years before their eventual conversions. Michael Low of Chebacco related that he was never under convictions until 1755 but that the earthquake of that year made him see the danger of his stubbornness of heart and enmity against God.[20] Lucy Proctor wrote, "In the time of the earthquake . . . I was bro't to see I hung over hell by the slender thread of life, and had done nothing but sin all my life,"[21] and Merriam Marcy of Sturbridge related, "What increased my anxiety was an earthquake last spring when God . . . shook terribly the earth in his anger. Had I been swallowed up in the belly of the earth God would have been just and I miserable."[22] Others saw God's wrath in storms. The wife of Moses Holbrook wrote, "it has pleased all mytey God to a waking me by thunder many a time which is terrifying to me and puts me in mind of my duty,"[23] and Hannah Heaton remembered the impression that lightning had made upon her as a child:

Now about this time i being i believe about thirteen years old i have lain awake all night for fear of the devil near this time them lights was seen often in the north sometimes it seemed almost as if there was living shapes of men in the air in arms moving after each other about half the orrisen lookt red like blood i was in dreadful distress of soul as if i was in a scorching fever some said it was a sign of a storm and it was imprest upon my mind that it was a storm of God's wrath a coming on the wicked world and it seemed as if I stood naked as it were to it.[24]

Themes of Conversions: The Fear of Death

Eighteenth-century New Englanders, like people of many other societies of the time, were surrounded by death and aware of its constant threat. Infant and child mortality was particularly high, and even if one survived childhood, death from disease or in childbirth was commonplace. The matter-of-factness with which converts mentioned the deaths that had punctuated their lives testifies to the omnipresence of death in this society and its importance in shaping the way in which people saw the world around them and thought about their own lives. Calvinism reinforced this awareness of death and invested it with a particular meaning: ministers routinely urged their congregations to remember that they might die at any time, to be continually prepared to face God.[25] Jemima Harding of Sturbridge at the age of twenty-eight had already seen many people close to her die. In her conversion account she spoke at length of these deaths and their impact upon her:

God was pleased to alarm me by the Death of sum of my near relations and acquaintance and about three years ago God was pleased to visit me with Sickness. At sich time and Since the Concerns of my soul lay with greater weight upon my mind than Ever before. . . . God was pleased to make a wonderful discovery to me of his compassion to me a poor sinfull creater that he was really a very present help in time of trouble and he was willing not only to grant me a safe deliverance in child bearing but to deliver me from my state of sin and misery. . . . Since I meet with that sore trial the loss of my first born I have a sense how fadeing and uncertain all things in this world are. I have seen more of that divine beauty and excellency there is in God and my soul cleaves more unto God.[26]

Such awareness of mortality led to conviction of sin and fear of hell, and the resulting anguish impelled some to think of suicide. Occasionally, a person was driven by despair to take his or her own life. But most, when their anguish became so deep that they felt they could no longer bear it, found the burden of sin falling off their shoulders and believed, to their profound relief, that Christ had interceded in their behalf and that God had granted forgiveness. Elizabeth Marshall wrote, "I saw Christ was willing but if I had been willing, but now I was willing. My Burden went off and my soul was filled with love to Christ and hatred of all sin . . . and afterwards I saw Christ was mine and I was his."[27] Jacob Choate wrote, "O damnation appeared intolerable and yet I saw it would be quite just in God to cast me down to Hell . . . and I have all out to him and found peace in my soul."[28] Jeremiah Kinsman of Chebacco recounted that during the revival he had become aware of his indifference to religion and saw himself condemned. One night he recalled, "as I was at home in my bed I had a view of the love of Christ and how ready and willing God was to be reconciled to me. . . . this view broke my heart to pieces to think what a rebellious creature I had been, how I had been sinning against a holy and kind God."[29] Mary Shumway described her ecstasy upon finding herself saved:

One night as I lay in Bed the Voice of the Son of God seemed to sound in my ears Saying Come unto me . . . take my yoak upon you and learn of my love I am meek

and lowly of heart and you shall find rest upon which many temptations seemed to
file away and my fears vanished as a shadow and Peace of Mind seemed to be my
Portion. . . . Whereas I was once blind I hope I now See.[30]

For both men and women, salvation meant rescue from chaos and hell,
heaven a refuge from danger. And for many of them there was a thin line
between the immediate dangers of the world around them and the ultimate
dangers of damnation: they saw the embers of hell in their own fireplaces
and God's wrath in thunder and lightning. This was good Calvinism, for it
was a tenet of Puritan belief that the physical world was full of lessons,
emblems, and signs of God's disposition toward his people. This overwhelming concern with mortality and the dangers of the natural world also
reflected the realities of life in eighteenth-century New England. Storms,
earthquakes, and disease killed people suddenly and inexplicably. These
people's lives were shaped in large measure by forces that they could neither
understand nor control; for many conversion was an opportunity to face the
fears that such powerlessness engendered and, at least temporarily, to allay
those fears through the hope of salvation.

The central themes of eighteenth-century conversions, guilt over
worldliness and fears of death and damnation, were expressed by both men
and women, and often they were expressed in very similar ways. In rural
colonial New England men and women faced many of the same concerns,
and in important ways they faced them together.

Men and women did different kinds of work and performed different
roles in their families and outside them, but they were united in a common
effort, pitted together against an often harsh and unpredictable natural
world. A rough equality between the sexes was fostered by common participation in a household economy that was to a large extent independent of the
market, and also by the near-frontier conditions of life. As long as families
lived close to the edge of survival everyone's labor was valued. The economic
and social centrality of the family within this society tended to elevate the
position of women, without whom, after all, family life would not have been
possible. Puritan theology involved a hierarchical view of society, and within
that hierarchy women were understood to be subordinate to men. But the
idea of subordination carried different connotations in Puritan society than it
would in later American history: worldly subordination was linked to
obedience to God, which was in turn linked to salvation. Puritan women

were not necessarily humiliated or devalued in the eyes of others because of their subordination to their husbands.

The Puritan Ideal: An Ordered Society

Calvinism was understood by Puritans, both ministry and laity, as implying a corporate, hierarchical theory of society. The Puritan oligarchy and ministry sought to build a stable and harmonious society, one dedicated to serving God and one in which they would be accepted as the interpreters of God's will. These men believed that the society that would best serve God was one that was arranged in an orderly and, in their view, therefore hierarchical manner, each rank overseeing the rank below it, each person obeying those above and holding authority over those below. Puritan ideology placed the subordination of wives to husbands in a larger context in which children obeyed their parents, lay adults obeyed the minister and the courts, and all New Englanders but especially the Puritan leadership obeyed God. According to Puritan theory, God had ordained that there be ranks and divisions in society so that there might be harmony and cooperation. While on board the *Arbella,* John Winthrop, soon to be governor of the Massachusetts Bay Colony, wrote:

God Almightie in His most holy and wise providence has so disposed of the Condition of mankind, as in all times some must be rich some poor, some high and eminent in power and dignitaries; others mean and in subjection . . . that every man might have need of the other, and hence they might be all knit more nearly together in the Bond of Brotherly affection.[31]

The primary goal of the Puritan leaders was the creation of such a community, one bound together by people's need for one another and dedicated to serving God. Such selflessness and cooperation, they believed, could result only from the mutual dependence of all members of society; furthermore, they believed that this mutuality required a division of social functions and an ordering of social status, as between parents and children. Puritan ministers often used the analogy of the body in speaking of society, pointing out that each limb and organ had a different function and that each needed every other. Jonathan Edwards explained the basis of cooperation in these terms: "If a multitude would help one another in any affair," he wrote, "they must unite themselves one to another in a regular subordination of members, in some measure, as it is in the natural body."[32]

This commitment to social hierarchy had been shaped in part by the Puritans' origins in England: they had formulated their views of social relations in a society of sharply defined classes, in which any challenge to the system of class meant a challenge to order. The relatively comfortable artisans, farmers, and merchants who made up the Puritan movement, and especially the elite who constituted its leadership, had little desire to criticize the class system and a large stake in the preservation of social order.

The Puritans' sense that order rested in inequalities of status and power was also rooted in their understanding of Calvinism. At the heart of the Puritan cosmology was a series of stark moral opposites: human degeneracy and divine holiness; the despair of sinners and the hopes of the saved; the forces of good and the forces of evil. The Puritans' focus on opposites and inequalities was strengthened by their reading of the theologian Peter Ramus, whose logic rested on a series of "positive contraries," categories that implied and required the existence of their opposites: hot could not exist without cold, or husband without wife. These contraries might be unequal in value, but they were necessarily complementary: each set made up a stable unit. The Puritan ministers who read Ramus found in his works a logical basis for their view that hierarchy and rank were the bases of social order.[33]

The implications of Puritan theology and social thought were mixed for women, but in the context of the seventeenth century they must be seen as on balance positive. Puritan New England was part of a larger European, and especially English, culture in which men were dominant. While Puritanism provided a justification for granting men a superior position and for regarding women's subordination as necessary, the Puritan corporate view of society validated the role of subordinate groups, such as women, and insisted that the subordinate had rights that must be respected by those in more powerful positions. In seventeenth-century Essex County, Massachusetts, one man was brought to court and fined on the basis of neighbors' reports that he had told his wife that she was "but his Servant."[34] The rigidly ordered Puritan world view did not permit women to achieve social equality with men, but it gave women some defense against any lowering of their position. Puritanism validated women in another important way, by setting salvation above gender. Visible sainthood, that is, evidence of an orthodox conversion and membership in the church, was held to be the most important criterion of status in Puritan society and probably was, in fact, in most communities, at least until the end of the seventeenth century. Women attained sainthood at least as frequently as men. The fact that sex was not a bar to sainthood, and that women attained it as often as they did, was an important guarantor of respect for women in Puritan society.[35]

Puritanism gave women reason to take pride in themselves as Christians, as contributing members of a society dedicated to serving God; it approved faith and service and looked with suspicion on worldly ambition, a temptation much more open to men than to women. The Puritan view of wealth was ambivalent: on the one hand work was respected, and prosperity arising from work was seen as a sign of God's favor and an opportunity to do good. But wealth itself was no proof of either virtue or divine approval: virtue lay in accepting one's station in life and making the best use of it. One minister wrote, "As Riches are not Evidence of God's love, so neither is Poverty of His Anger or Hatred; being such things in themselves make Men neither better nor worse, and are equally improvable for Eternal Salvation."[36] Though the ministry endorsed efforts to bring prosperity to New England as a whole, they condemned the pursuit of self-interest for its own sake. In 1728 one minister warned his congregation: "There is nothing renders a Man more unlike God than a narrow contracted Spirit, whose Views terminate on his own dear self, and whose proper emblem is the Hedgehog, who wraps itself up in its own soft down, and turns out brizzils to all the World besides."[37]

The Goal of the Church: A Corporate Community

The church's hostility to individualism, especially to individual pursuit of gain at the expense of others, reflected its commitment to maintaining a hierarchical and traditional society. The main opposition that the church faced in this regard came from the merchants, who had no coherent ideology in opposition to Puritanism, were in most cases themselves church members, but often found themselves in conflict with church and state. In 1639, Robert Keayne, a Boston merchant, was tried and convicted for "oppression," the making of excessive profits in trade. He was fined by the court and censured by the church, and John Cotton, the Boston minister, took the opportunity to outline "false" and "true" principles of trade. Among the practices that he condemned were the following:

1. That a man might sell as dear as he can, and buy as cheap as he can.
2. If a man lose by casualty of sea, etc., in some of his commodities, he may raise the price of the rest.
3. That, as a man may take the advantage of his own skill or ability, so he may of another's ignorance or necessity.[38]

The Puritan state as well as the church was committed to placing the interests of the community ahead of the aspirations of individuals. Especially in the first several decades of settlement, before the merchant class had become strong enough to sway public policy, the courts did not hesitate to put these traditionalist principles into practice by regulating trade that they saw as posing a threat to the Puritan community.

In the early 1640s, for instance, rumors circulated in New England that the English Civil War might disrupt trade with New England, cutting off the importation of essential goods. Courts throughout New England responded to these rumors by setting maximum prices on imported goods so as to prevent merchants from benefiting from a panic. Even in the eighteenth century, when the merchants had gained the balance of political power in the provincial councils, Puritan attitudes could still influence the courts to prohibit trade that might produce distress. In 1725, at a time when grain was in short supply in New England, the Bay Colony Council received a complaint that two ships were being loaded with corn in the Boston harbor, preparing to sail for England. The council ordered that the ships be unloaded, that the corn be sold "for the supply of the Townes," and that henceforth no one "presume" to export grain without the permission of the council.[39]

Such actions expressed one side of Puritan corporatism: its emphasis on social responsibility. The other side of that corporate ideology was authoritarianism: the insistence on deference, on the obedience of inferiors to superiors. Both of these attitudes were deeply embedded in New Englanders, inculcated in children at home and in school as well as in church, and reinforced by community pressure in adulthood. Children were taught from infancy to obey their parents in every particular; from the age of six or seven on they were expected to put the interests of their families ahead of their own inclinations and to work long hours along with parents and older brothers and sisters. These lessons were reinforced in the Puritan schools, for those children who attended them: the first message of the *New England Primer* was obedience, and the second was mutual love and assistance. The opening sentences of "The Dutiful Child's Promises," the first entry in the primer after the alphabet, read:

I will fear God, and honour the KING
I will honour my Father and Mother.
I will Obey my Superiors.
I will Submit to my Elders.
I will Love my Friends.
I will hate no Man.
I will forgive my Enemies, and Pray to God for Them.[40]

Over the seventeenth and eighteenth centuries, the hold of this ideology probably weakened somewhat throughout New England: as the merchant class grew and gained prestige and power, and as the market spread through large areas of the countryside, it became increasingly difficult for the church to restrain individual ambition. In Boston especially the hold of the church was weakened: growing trade and industry attracted large numbers of immigrants who came for the economic opportunities the city offered and not out of devotion to Puritanism. The more people crowded into Boston, the harder it was for the churches to maintain their hold even over those of Puritan background. But in the countryside the church and Puritan ideology continued to be strong. Though there was some gradual falling off of church membership and attendance, the spread of the Great Awakening through the countryside was evidence of how much guilt had attended this drift away from the church and of the extent to which, whether in or out of the church, rural New Englanders held to the old religious world view. During the Great Awakening, the common people not only reaffirmed their belief in the traditional values but outdid their ministers in their adherence to them. In many communities prorevival parishioners accused ministers of insufficient orthodoxy, especially of a tendency to moderate the wrath of God in their preaching, to exaggerate the ability of Christians to prepare the way for salvation through their actions. New Englanders might have drifted away from the church, but they seem to have clung to the old ideas, especially the authoritarianism of orthodox Puritanism.[41]

Puritan ideology had its uses for both rulers and ruled—for the Puritan oligarchy, the ministry, and the common people. The beliefs that New England was a holy commonwealth dedicated to the service of God and that such service required obedience to authority and selfless cooperation among the people probably helped to create a stable community and certainly reinforced the authority of the Puritan oligarchy and of the local ministry. These ideas also helped to invest meaning in New Englanders' drab and arduous lives and gave them fortitude in the early years of struggle with the wilderness and fear of the Indians. This ideology was compatible with life on the family farm and probably helped it to run smoothly; it reinforced the authority of parents (especially fathers), stressed cooperation, and affirmed the importance of everyone's contribution, including that of women and children. It admonished inferiors—servants, children, women—to stay in their places and reminded them that in spite of their inferior rank they too might be among the elect if their faith and obedience were sufficient.

This outlook survived largely intact in much of New England well into the eighteenth century because it helped people to understand their own lives, because it was socially useful, especially for those in positions of authority, and because there was no clear challenge to it. Nevertheless, it was not an accurate description of New England life even in the countryside, and its deficiencies became more glaring over time. First, New England life was never as hierarchical as Puritan theory proclaimed. The conditions of the frontier made for a great deal of economic equality among settling families, and while economic distinctions were always present and growing sharper, until well into the eighteenth century there were few New Englanders outside the tiny Boston aristocracy who did not have to work with their hands. On the family farm, the importance of women's work increased women's power considerably above that prescribed by Puritan theory. In Boston there were rich and poor from the beginning, and class differences increased over time, but these divisions did little to reinforce Puritanism or the authority of the ministry, it was in the more economically egalitarian towns that Puritan authority endured. This deficiency in Puritan theory was not fatal; people could enjoy a greater degree of equality than their ideology allowed for without rejecting that ideology as long as it explained to them why they had to defer to others as much as they did and reassured them of their worth in spite of their subordination.

The real weakness of Puritan ideology was that it was incompatible with trade relations. In the eighteenth century the internal New England market was growing rapidly and drawing increasing numbers of people, most of them farmers, into its web. The Puritan stress on deference and cooperation was useful on the family farm, especially if it was at or near the level of subsistence and operating in a barter economy in which people traded not for profit but because they could not themselves make everything they needed. As the market system developed, however, it presented New Englanders, especially men, with opportunities for profit that required the aggressive self-assertion and pursuit of self-interest that Puritanism condemned. It was largely trade that drew New Englanders, especially men, away from church membership and church attendance. The tenets of Puritanism did not mix well with the necessities of the market. Puritan ministers saw trade and religion as competing with one another and were afraid that trade would win the contest. In 1963, one minister wrote:

My fathers and Brethren, this is never to be forgotten, that New-England is originally a plantation of Religion, not a Plantation of Trade. Let Merchants and such as are increasing Cent per Cent remember this, Let others that have come over since at several times understand this, that worldly gain was not the end and design of the people of New England, but Religion. And if any man among us make Religion as twelve, and the World as thirteen, let such as one know he hath neither the spirit of a true New-England man, nor yet of a sincere Christian.[42]

The Puritans were right to fear the growth of trade: it threatened to undermine the power of the Puritan oligarchy and ministry and to bring into question the deference and social harmony that they espoused. The merchant class was a real threat to the Puritan oligarchy; in Boston it had managed to obtain the balance of power within half a century of settlement. Even in the countryside, where there was hardly a merchant class, trade disrupted Puritan norms of behavior and often church control as well. The subsistence farming that prevailed in most of rural New England throughout the colonial period favored cooperation, at least within the family. As some farms, especially those near the coast and along the Connecticut River, began to produce a surplus and sell it to Boston, New Haven, and the other towns, men were drawn into a market system that encouraged competition, aggressive self-interest, and greater attention to wordly success. The greater involvement of men than of women in trade was probably a major reason why eighteenth-century men left the church in greater numbers than women: in the market men would find a new social arena, and trade presented temptations that might undermine men's claim to salvation. Women continued to need the social life provided by the church, and their lives were more likely than men's to continue to be reasonably consistent with Puritan teachings.

Puritanism regarded the family as basic to social order but at the same time held relations within families to be relatively unproblematic: family hierarchies, Puritans tended to assume, were secured by tradition and habit and did not require the kind of reinforcement that hierarchy and order in society generally called for. In colonial New England there was little public discussion of the family or the role of women. Of the reams of literature published in New England in the seventeenth and eighteenth centuries, little touched on either topic. The ministers who wrote the didactic literature of the period, published in the form of sermons and tracts, assumed that people would marry and have children as a matter of course. One could hardly run a farm by oneself, and social life outside the family was virtually nonexistent. Young people tended to marry as soon as family obligations permitted, and any man or woman whose spouse died was likely to begin looking for a replacement within a matter of months.[43] For farming people of this time there was every incentive to marry, and every reason to hold a marriage together once it had been established.

The sparseness of printed material about the family in colonial New England indicates a confidence in its viability and an assumption that the roles of the sexes were fixed by God and nature and did not require discussion. But this complacency did not mean that the Puritans saw the family as unimportant; on the contrary, when they did discuss the family, it was often to point out how fundamental it was to Puritan society. Cotton Mather wrote, in one of the few Puritan tracts on family life, "As the Great God, who at the Beginning said, let us make man after our Image, so it is evident, that Families are the Nurseries of all Societies; and the first Combinations of Mankind. Well Ordered Families naturally produce a Good Order in other Societies."[44] The view that social order rested on the maintenance of the family was reflected in the Massachusetts regulation that married people who came to the colony must either bring their spouses and live with them or return home. Puritan law was shaped by the assumption that family discipline was the first and most effective instrument of social control: a disorderly person was likely to be placed by the court in a household of its choosing, under the authority of a husband and wife known for their moral behavior.[45]

Another indication of the importance that the Puritan leaders invested in the family lay in their scrutiny and control of family relations. Husbands and wives were forbidden by law to be unfaithful to one another, to desert, strike, or treat one another cruelly. The courts chastised, fined, and sometimes jailed transgressors; in extreme cases divorces might be granted. And such court action did not depend upon the complaint of the victim. If, for instance, it came to the attention of the court, perhaps through the reports of neighbors, that a husband had been beating or reviling his wife, the court was obliged to interfere even if the wife did not object to such treatment. In the eyes of the court, the man's behavior was a crime not only against his wife but against Puritan society as a whole, for by disrupting family life it threatened social order.[46] Furthermore, like any violation of God's law it was an invitation to divine judgment and retribution against the people of New England as a whole. For both of these reasons Puritan authorities saw it as their responsibility to establish standards of family relations and to chastise anyone who might violate them.

The ministerial sermons and tracts on family life were written in the attempt to define these standards, to describe the rights and duties of husbands and wives and of parents and children. In discussing the relationship of wives to husbands, these tracts tried to describe a balance between subordination and mutuality. Women were to obey their husbands, but husbands were reminded that women were not to be subjugated beyond certain limits. Benjamin Wadsworth, in his tract entitled *The Well-Ordered Family,* urged the husband not to demean his wife by overstepping the bounds of his authority. "Though he governs her, he must not treat her as a Servant, but as his *own Flesh*; he must love her as himself, Ephesians 5 : 33. He should strive to make his Government of her, as easie and gentle as possible; and strive more to be lov'd than fear'd; though neither is to be excluded." He went on to list the mutual obligations of wife and husband to one another:

1. Tis their duty to cohabit or dwell together with one another.
2. That they should have a very great and tender love and affection one to another.
3. They should be chaste, and faithful to one another.
4. Should be helpful to one another.
5. Should be patient one towards another.
6. Should honor one another.[47]

Puritanism and Women's Rights

The fact that women could bring their husbands to court for violating at least the more explicit of these standards is an indication of the relatively strong position of women in colonial New England. Women had more power, both legal and informal, there than elsewhere, and also more than they would hold in New England itself in the early nineteenth century.[48] Men and women were hardly equal in colonial New England: land, which was the primary basis of wealth, was overwhelmingly owned by men and was ordinarily handed down from father to sons, a practice reinforced by Puritan law, according to which any property a woman might inherit became the property of her husband at her marriage. But the law, like the ministerial tracts on family life, granted some limited rights to women within this framework of male dominance. If a woman's first husband were to die, she might retain ownership of any property she brought into a second marriage.[49] And within marriage itself she had some rights: her legal consent was necessary before her husband could place their child in another household as an apprentice or servant, a common practice in colonial New England; furthermore, according to a law adopted from the English tradition, a man was required to leave at least a third of his estate to his wife if she had done a normal amount of work and thus made a reasonable contribution to the prosperity of the family. Any will that did not meet this standard could be rectified by the court. Probably most important of all was the right of a woman to appear in court and speak in her own behalf, a right that married women would no longer possess by the nineteenth century.[50]

The tightness of community life in colonial New England, the Puritan view that everyone had a right to be concerned with what everyone else was doing, helped to give force to these standards of behavior within the family and therefore to give women more protection than they might have had in more loosely organized or more geographically dispersed communities, or in communities with a greater respect for family privacy. The physical advantages that men have over women, their tendency toward stronger musculature and their freedom from pregnancy, could not be used so freely against women when men had neighbors, relatives, and ultimately the court to answer to. In both the eighteenth and nineteenth centuries, women seem to have valued community ties highly, often more highly than men; women converts rejoiced to find themselves part of a community and sometimes described heaven as having the same conviviality as a revival. In the nineteenth century when families moved to frontier areas, it was women who complained most bitterly of isolation. This female emphasis on community was at least partly a result of the fact that women were more confined to the home than were men and therefore more cut off from adult company. But it may also have arisen in part from some sense of the importance of community ties to a woman's position in her own family.

The relations of parents and children, like those of husbands and wives, were subject to ministerial definition and public scrutiny in Puritan society. The fact that women were usually classed as "parents," along with their husbands, rather than as mothers in contrast to fathers, enhanced women's position in the family. Usually the authors of tracts on family life did not distinguish between the responsibilities of mothers and fathers but spoke simply of parental duties. When these authors did speak particularly of the relations of mothers and children, they were likely to do so in terms that could as easily have been applied to the relations of fathers and children. Benjamin Colman, an eighteenth-century minister, described the claims that a "vertuous woman" held upon the respect of her children:

Her children rise up and call her blessed. And this may signify and import . . . the Reverence that her children bear to her . . . her superior *Relations* to them, her *Age,* her *Wisdom,* and *Gravity,* her *Benefits* to them, and all her Personal Excellencies do command from them . . . for it is the First Commandment with Promise, Honour thy Father and thy Mother.[51]

The relations of Puritan women to their children were different from those of fathers to children in important ways. Puritan women not only gave birth but nursed babies and had primary responsibility for keeping an eye on small children. But childbirth and nursing were natural functions and probably did not seem to these ministers to require any special instruction; the lack of discussion of any special maternal responsibility for child care probably reflected the absence of a strict division between the sexes here, for on these family farms men often looked after children. As soon as boys began working in the fields with their fathers, women were relieved of much of the responsibility for looking after them, and in the winter months, when everyone in the family worked or played in the main room of the house, the father's authority was as immediate as the mother's.

In the nineteenth and twentieth centuries women and children have come to be regarded as comprising one large social category set apart from men. This attitude was not part of Puritan thinking: in Puritan literature on the family, the most important distinction was between children and adults. The relatively good position of women in this society was not shared by their children, who were expected to submit without question to the authority of their parents; often such deference was expected from adult as well as minor children. Ministers outlined a stark inequality between parents and children: parents were to care for their children's physical needs, discipline them, and train them to be good Christians and good citizens: children were obliged to respect and obey their parents. Cotton Mather wrote, "The Respects that Children must render unto their Parents, are Comprized in those Three Words, Reverence, and Obedience, and Recompense."[52]

In this relation there was to be no mutuality, no approach toward equality. This authoritarianism was reinforced by Puritan law, according to which disobedient children could be punished by the court with extreme severity; the law provided for the execution of such children, though there do not seem to have been any cases in which this sentence was carried out. Parents as well as the courts seem to have believed that severity was necessary in the raising of children. Puritans who wrote about parenthood stressed the importance of discipline, and one historian has suggested that the Puritan custom of placing children in other households as servants or apprentices may have been motivated at least in part by parents' fears that they would be too lenient with their own children.[53]

The lot of Puritan children was certainly not enhanced by the sharp division that was drawn between their status and that of adults; women, on the other hand, derived benefits from the fact that their special connection with children was given less emphasis in this society than in many others, that their roles were defined as adults and parents as well as mothers. The nineteenth-century cult of motherhood constituted a gain for women in some limited ways: the sanctification of motherhood gave women a new kind of leverage within their families and, ultimately, a platform from which to speak on social issues. But the cost of the nineteenth-century absorption of woman into the role of mother was her loss of prestige or power in any other role. In a society in which family life was increasingly separate from and marginal to economic life and political power, that loss was serious.

The Colonial Farm Woman

The lack of sex barriers to salvation in a society so concerned with religion undoubtedly enhanced women's position; but the fundamental reason for women's relatively good position in this society, and for the relative lack of distinction made between masculine and feminine roles, was the importance of women in the family economy on which the society was based. In a society in which land was relatively easy to acquire but could not be utilized without family labor, men and women were in important ways dependent upon one another.

The role of women in colonial New England families and society seems to have been one of greater strength than that outlined by the ministers in their descriptions of family life. And certainly these women commanded greater respect than an account of women drawn from the Bible would have suggested. Even Cotton Mather, who was often uneasy about women and especially about female sexuality, noted with some surprise that the role of women in the Holy Commonwealth was not what he would have expected from the daughters of Eve. In trying to account for the high repute of so many New England women, he recalled the burdens that they bore:

I have seen it without going a Mile from Home, that in a Church of between three or four hundred Communicants, there are but few more than one hundred Men, all the rest are Women, of whom Charity will think no Evil. Possibly, one reason for it is, there are more Women in the World than Men, but this is not all the Reason. It seems that the Curse in the Difficulties both of Subjection and of Childbearing, which the Female Sex is doomed unto, has been turned into a blessing.[54]

As Mather pointed out, these women's lives were hard. They were filled not only with the difficulties of childbirth but with continual and strenuous physical labor as well. Hard work need not be the basis for status: the more stratified a society, the more the reverse is likely to be the case. But in New England's relatively simple society, in the context of a near-subsistence economy, work and the contribution to welfare that it brought were more likely to elicit respect than to be seen as a sign of social inferiority. Work could mean low status only in a class society in which the wealth and high status of some were based on the work and poverty of others. In the rural communities of colonial New England people lived mostly from their own labor; the development of classes was only beginning. In this context women's labor was held in respect.

Femininity as we understand it played little role in these women's lives or in the Puritan conception of woman's role. Puritan women were told to obey their husbands, but the social graces and childlike innocence that later came to be associated with womanhood had little place on the New England farm. Puritan women were urged to exercise moral authority in their homes, but in this regard ministers addressed them as Christian adults and parents, and not particularly as women. The austere Puritan conception of womanhood was compatible with the way women lived in the New England countryside; but in the cities life was different, and the upper class, at least, began to formulate new ideas of femininity.

The Upper-Class Lady

In urban communities, the role of women was becoming an issue by the late eighteenth century. Women, and perhaps men as well, began to read books, often imported from England, that described the lady and offered instruction toward becoming one. These books were the first genre of literature read widely in New England that indicated distinct models of masculinity and femininity. One author described the difference between the two:

Women's brows were not intended to be ploughed with wrinkles, nor their innocent gaiety damped by abstraction. They were perpetually to please, and perpetually to enliven. If we were to plan the *edifice*, they were to furnish the *embellishments*. If we were to lay out and cultivate the garden, they were to beautifully *fringe* its borders with flowers. If we were to superintend the management of kingdoms, they were to be the fairest ornaments of those kingdoms, the embellishers of society, and the sweeteners of life.[55]

This concept of womanhood, shaped by the experience of the English upper classes, was attainable by at least some women of the merchant class, especially at its upper levels. Such women could be supported by their husbands, had a fair amount of time for social life, and could send their daughters to academies where their education included decorative arts and their social graces could be polished. This style of femininity had no relevance for the farm women who, in the late eighteenth century, still made up the vast majority of New England's female population. It did have some relevance for another group of women just beginning to emerge within New England: women of the newly developing commercial towns, who were not wealthy but who, as their husbands turned away from farming and toward trades and professions, found themselves less involved in the production of goods and increasingly involved in domesticity, the care of children, husbands, and home. These women, like the wealthy ladies of the cities, faced the question of how to construct new roles for themselves. For this group, however, the central concern was how to be a good mother rather than how to be a good hostess. A literature directed toward these women, equivalent to the late eighteenth-century literature for the lady, was not to appear until after the turn of the nineteenth century.

For the vast majority of New England women through the eighteenth century, neither the definition of femininity nor the question of relations between the sexes seems to have been a pressing issue. Revivals, especially when they occur during or in the wake of a social upheaval as massive as the Great Awakening, allow poeple not only to give voice to their everyday concerns but also to raise, at least indirectly, issues that in normal times remain buried. The Great Awakening temporarily removed some of the constraints that governed everyday life in eighteenth-century New England. During a revival people might cry out during church meetings; they might drop their work to pray or to gather with others who were also under conviction. Converts might burst into tears at unexpected moments or embrace one another in the streets. While the revival lasted, it allowed those who took part in it some space in which to throw aside routine, to disregard the pressures of work that ordinarily structured their lives. During the revival, questions of authority were also likely to be raised. God's authority was a central issue of conversion for both men and women. On a more mundane level, the relations between laity and clergy could be strengthened, restructured, or broken, depending upon the minister's attitude toward the revival and his congregation's ability to exercise power over him. As congregations put pressure on their ministers to conform to their views of piety, or in extreme cases left them to form new churches, questions of authority and deference were at least temporarily recast in New England.

In this context it is striking that the question of men's power over women seems in no way to have come to the surface in these revivals, or to have been raised even indirectly in the course of women's conversions.

Though women participated in the Great Awakening and in the revivals that followed it in at least as large numbers as men, they do not seem to have seized upon an atmosphere of social disorder as an opportunity to redefine their roles as women, or to have found in conversion a chance to vent frustrations resulting from their subservience to men. Though these eighteenth-century revivals were social upheavals of much greater magnitude than the revivals of the early nineteenth century would be, they did not contain the elements of female protest that would be present later. The fact that the role of women did not become an issue in the revivals and conversions of the Great Awakening suggests that male domination was not widely experienced by women as an issue in their lives; the subordination of women was of a piece with Puritan thought as a whole and did not seem to impede the functioning of family economy, or society more generally. Inequality between the sexes was not yet objectionable either in theory or in practice.

The religious converison narratives of Puritan men and women were striking for the similarities of their concerns and their language, but it is possible to find some patterns of difference between the sexes in these narratives as well. These differences, subtle as they were, are worth examination, for they foreshadowed the much greater divergence that would appear in the nineteenth century. Women often expressed more profound guilt and sharper fears of death than men, and their relief upon conversion often seemed keener. Women's greater fears may have been rooted partly in biological experience. At every childbirth a woman risked her life, and special involvement with infants, who in the eighteenth century often did not survive their early years, brought women especially close to the issue of mortality.

In addition to such differences in tone, there were also subtle differences in the degree of emphasis that men and women gave to the various issues raised by the conversion experience. Though men and women both angrily resisted conversion at first, once they began to think about their sins men were more likely to emphasize particular misdeeds, women to emphasize original sin. Among the Chebacco converts three men and one woman gave overwhelming weight to their actual sins; four women and one man spoke primarily of original sin. Among the remaining thirty-four, men were more likely to emphasize their sinful deeds, women to condemn their very beings—though both sexes spoke of both categories of sin. Men, in speaking of their actual sins, occasionally used phrases that suggested that they might have in mind their pursuit of material gain. Isaac Proctor of Chebacco wrote, "I see that God might justly have cutt me off while I was in the pursuits of this world,"[56] and John Lendal was struck by a biblical phrase that compared earthly to spiritual profits. He recounted:

I have been not only a person devoid of Religion but of Morality, and a great opposer of the work of God going on among us. And was under no concern until I heard Mr. Cleaveland preach about those words, what will it profit a man if he should gain the whole world and lose his soul.—What he said of sinners being punished for ever struck my heart. . . . I was brought to see the wrath of God was out against me and I was in immediate danger of stepping into the flames of Hell.[57]

Women, when they did speak of immorality, often mentioned their former disinterest in religion or their frivolity; Hannah Heaton, for instance, wrote:

I went to frolickes all winter and stifled the conviction I had of its being a soul ruining sin i was much for fine cloaths and fashins . . . [on election day, in Middletown] i was at a tavern in a frolick there come in a young man . . . and told me how the work of god was carried on there and of several of my mates that was converted.[58]

In general, women did not dwell upon their worldly behavior but rather focused on the state of their souls. Bethiah Foster wrote, "My original sins which I bro't with me into the world appeared so great, that I thought all my actual sins were as nothing compared to them."[59] The two conversions that John Cleaveland, the Chebacco minister, quoted in his account of the revival in his congregation neatly exemplify this difference between the concerns that women and men brought to the conversion experience. The young man whose experience he related emphasized the guilt he felt over his worldly sins, saying, "My conscience began to be stirred and told me I had lived a careless life, and had been pursuing the World and the Things of Time and Sense, and had no reason to think but that I was in a State of Nature." The young woman also spoke of her worldly behavior, but instead of pointing to her sins in the world she emphasized her mistake in believing that moral behavior was enough: "I went about to establish a Righteousness of my own, and so settled down upon a sandy Foundation . . . I was bro't to see, I was deceiving myself with a false Hope, and was in Danger of perishing with a Lie in my right Hand." She had a sharp sense of her original sin:

It pleased God . . . to open my View to that Fountain of Sin that was in my Heart, and give me to see that I had sinned in my first Father Adam, and . . . that my Nature was full of Sin, and that it would be just with God to lay upon me the Punishment of my Sin, which would be eternal Damnation.[60]

Women's conversion accounts also differed from those of men in that women in speaking of their sins were prone to condemn themselves profusely and generally, to describe themselves much more harshly than men described themselves. Sarah Putridge of Sturbridge wrote of herself, "Of all creatures I was the most ungrateful and the most undeserving of any grace."[61] Lucy Allins wrote, "I have been . . . made sensible I deserved nothing but God's wrath and curse and that forever which made me to look back on the evil of my ways and the wickedness of my being which made my life appear like one Act of Sin. And that I had done nothing but Sin against a holy god all my days."[62] And Jemima Harding recounted, "I had . . . a sense of ye wonderful goodness of God to me a Poor Sinful Creater and of my own sinfulness, vileness, and unworthyness."[63] Chebacco women used similar language. Lucy Proctor wrote, "I was bro't to see I hung over Hell by the slender thread of life, and had done nothing but sin all my life. . . . I loathe sins and myself with perfect hatred."[64] And Hannah Heaton wrote of having for a time put off thinking about religion because examining her heart "made me feel so ugly."[65] None of the men in these accounts used such language in speaking of himself.

Both men and women, when they felt themselves to be in God's presence, felt awed and unworthy. But women were likely to express this sense more strongly than did men, and they did so in terms of a feeling of impurity in contrast to God's holiness. Jonathan Edwards recalled talking with a woman who was undergoing conversion. She seemed "overborne and sinking; and when she could speak expressing in a manner that can't be described the sense she had of the glory of God . . . and her own unworthiness, her longing to lie at the dust.[66] Nathan Cole, on the other hand, felt insignificant but by no means debased when he found himself in God's presence. He wrote:

God appeared unto me and made me Shringe; before whose face the heavens and the earth fled away; and I was shrinked into a nothing; I knew not whether I was in the body or not, I seemed to hang in the air before God, and he seemed to speak to me in an angry and Sov'n way, what won't you trust your soul with God. My heart answered, O yes, yes . . . [67]

All converts, male and female, were required to examine their thoughts and feelings closely, but it was women who were most likely to dwell upon evil thoughts. Hannah Heaton, for instance, described a thought as "the unpardonable sin." She wrote:

Once I had a doleful blasphemous thought about Christ cast into my mind I was terrifyed with it and feard it was the unpardonable sin. . . . It would sometimes dart into my mind with such power it would make me cry out sometimes I used to get it out of my mind by saying the lord's prayer or by thinking of some good thoughts as I called them after a while I told a friend of mine of it privately and I was delivered at once.[68]

Nathan Cole told of another woman, a close friend of his, who was thrown into consternation by an evil thought. She had undergone what he regarded as "a very clear gospel Conversion," but, he wrote,

after a few weeks Satan comes . . . with a drove of temptations and horrible thoughts, and threw them into her mind, and then told her she was a dreadful Sinner to have such thoughts and blasphemous temptations against God, they are dreadful Sins says he, and you are no Christian because you have such temptations; she labored under these things for some time and at length told me; and here I had a very close dispute with Satan . . . as he put these things into her mind so she spake them unto me. . . . Satan all the while said they were her sins, and strove to prove it by scripture, but I proved by scripture they were not hers. I told her . . . if her heart strove against them they were not her sins.[69]

Perhaps these obsessive thoughts involved sexual impulses, possibly directed toward God or Christ and the fathers or other males that these religious figures stood for unconsciously. But such feelings, even if present in the cases of these two women, were evidently not common. Other women converts did not allude to such concerns. Sexual fantasies seem not to have been ordinarily a part, or at least a conscious part, of the conversion experience.

Calvinism and the Inferiority of Women

The different concerns of Puritan men and women can be understood in the context of the differences in their lives and the inferiority of women within Puritan thought. Though women came closer to equality with men in eighteenth-century New England than they did later, they were nevertheless treated as men's inferiors and taught to regard themselves as such. Calvinism granted women respect as long as they stayed in the position assigned them. That position, however, was a subordinate one, and such subordination was justified by a belief in women's inferiority. The tendency of eighteenth-century women to judge themselves with special harshness, their propensity to see themselves as imbued with sin regardless of their actions, reflected the view of women held by the society in which they lived. Puritanism viewed all human beings as evil, but it tended to view women as especially so. The conversion accounts of men and women reflected this difference.

Calvinism required equal obligations of men and women in the duties of religious devotion and obedience to God, but it did not consider them to be equal in the world; though both were to manifest their piety by humility and by obedience to worldly authorities, women were expected to obey more authorities than men and to assume a special degree of humility. Men were required to obey church and secular authorities; women were to obey their husbands as well. Ministers, in sermons and tracts, reminded women of their subordinate status. Benjamin Wadsworth, an early eighteenth-century minister, wrote in a treatise directed to women: "The Husband is called the Head of the Woman (I Corinthians 11:3). It belongs to the Head, to rule and govern." In his view the subordination of the wife to her husband was inherent in her role and did not depend upon the personal qualities of either husband or wife. He continued:

Those wives are much to blame, who don't carry it lovingly and obediently toward their own Husbands. . . . Though possibly thou hast greater abilities of mind than he has, wast of some high birth, and he of a more Mean Extract; or didst bring more estate at Marriage than he did; yet since he is thy Husband, God has made him thy head, and set him over thee.[70]

Most Puritan ministers assumed that though a few women might be superior in some respects to particular men, women's abilities on the whole were lesser. An extreme example of Puritan misogyny was John Winthrop's comment upon hearing that the wife of Governor Hopkins of Connecticut had become insane. "If she had attended to her household affairs," he wrote, "and such things as belong to women, and had not gone out of her way and calling to meddle in such things as are proper for men, whose minds are stronger, etc., she had kept her wits.[71]

The view that eighteenth-century New England women held of themselves was shaped not only by the general notion of women's inferiority but also by the idea that while all people were naturally depraved women were likely to be especially so. Every New England schoolchild knew that it was Eve who had tempted Adam and that it was therefore Eve who held ultimate responsibility for the Fall. Puritan ministers were given to reminding women of the special onus that lay upon them because of this, their special responsibility for the taint that this disobedient act had brought upon the human race and upon carnality itself. The notion that women were especially accountable for lost innocence was easily translated into an idea that sexuality was somehow especially connected with women. This sexualized attitude toward women is evident in Puritan ministers' remarks about their congregations' style of dress. Occasional ministers warned men against dressing ostentatiously, but the reasons they gave had little to do with sexuality. Solomon Stoddard, for instance, in condemning men's wearing of periwigs, made the following objections:

1. It is an *Uncontentedness* with the Provision that God has made for man. . . .
2. It is *Wastefulness.* Abundance of Money is *needlessly* spent in maintaining this *Practice.*
3. It is *Pride*; they do it to make a great Show. . . .
4. It is *contrary to Gravity.*

Only incidentally, at the end of his discussion, did he mention the sexual aspect of men's dress. The wearing of periwigs, he wrote, "makes [men] look, as if they were more disposed to Court a Maid; than to bear upon their Hearts the weighty Concernments of God's Kingdom."[72]

Women were more likely to be lectured about their dress than were men, and when ministers lectured women on this topic they tended to focus on the question of sexuality. They spoke of "immodest" dress and of physical attractiveness as a snare for men. Cotton Mather, for instance, denounced cosmetics as "the guise of an Harlot. A painted face," he wrote, "is but a painted Sign hung out for advice to Strangers, that they shall find Entertainment there." And he saw male sexual desires as the fault of the women toward whom they were directed. "For the Nakedness of the Back and Breasts," he wrote, "no Reason can be given; unless it be that a Woman by showing a fair Skin enkindle a foul Fire in the Male Spectators."[73]

Eighteenth-century women, as we have seen, showed greater religiosity than men, greater involvement in Calvinism and in the conversion experience. They also expressed a particularly sharp pleasure in the sense of community created by a revival. Men enjoyed this aspect of revivals as well; both male and female converts spoke of being filled with a sudden and intense love for "God's people" upon their own conversions, and observers wrote of entire communities rejoicing in a spirit of sisterhood and brotherhood. A participant described a revival in Portsmouth, Connecticut, in the following terms:

Ye Spirit of God don't seem confined to any but all in general are partaking. . . . It was excellently told by ye Apostle John 4 : 16. Whoever dwelleth in God dwelleth in love. This is fulfilled of a truth. High and low rich and poor white and black all are rejoicing together in Christ and are not afraid to call one another Brother and Sister.[74]

Though men as well as women took part in such rejoicing, accounts of individual conversions indicate that women experienced particularly intense love toward others, converts especially but sometimes "sinners" as well, and took particular delight in the new community of which they found themselves a part. Jonathan Edwards wrote of a young woman convert who "told one of her sisters . . . that she loved all mankind but especially the people of God." Three recent converts entered the shop where she was working; this "so affected her, that she almost fainted."[75] Martha Andrews of Chebacco recounted that, upon conversion, "I found love of God and Delight on God's word and compassions to the perishing sinner, that I thought I could even be ready to die for them."[76] Some converts, in the ecstasy of conversion, may not have distinguished between love of God and love of other people. John Cleaveland, the Chebacco minister, quoted a young woman's account of her feelings upon finding herself to be saved: she wrote, "I seemed to myself a little Mote, swallowed up in the Ocean of Love!"[77]

Conclusion

The lives of Puritan farm women were not shaped by modern notions of femininity or by the nineteenth-century sense of extreme polarization between male and female. Differences between men and women, either social or biological, were not, as they would later become, a major topic of public discussion. Nevertheless, close examination reveals some patterns of difference between men's and women's ways of describing their experiences. Neither side of this conclusion should be surprising. Puritans had little reason to stress sexual difference: it was a solid fact of biological and social life. The division of labor between men and women was rooted in century upon century of tradition and bolstered by what at least appeared to be the practical demands of farm life on the frontier. For these people, the division of labor between the sexes had the substantiality of a law of nature, requiring no special emphasis. It remained one of the fundamental structures of social life and as such shaped the experience and outlook of both sexes.[78]

CHAPTER TWO

Religious Conversions in the Nineteenth Century: Men's and Women's Diverging Experiences

THE REVIVALS of the 1760s were the last that New England was to see until nearly the turn of the century. What the clergy regarded as the excesses of the Great Awakening strengthened the arguments of those ministers who had opposed it from the beginning; by the time the Awakening died out, the majority of New England's clergy had become skeptical of revivals as a means of promoting religion and uneasy about popular, "enthusiastic" religion. In the last decades of the eighteenth century, many of the clergy who had been critical of the Awakening when it was taking place developed an increasingly rationalist outlook which, to the extent that it held sway in New England, tended to discourage revivalism. Meanwhile, conflict between the colonial elites and Britain and the movement for independence created a new focus and new outlets for popular discontent. Not until the Revolution was well in the past would religious revivalism again emerge on a large scale.

By 1797 revivals began to sweep through New England, as in the Great Awakening beginning in the Connecticut River Valley and spreading through the towns of Connecticut, Massachusetts, Rhode Island, western New York, and to some extent northern New England. Though geographically as widespread as the Great Awakening, these revivals were socially more limited. From the accounts of contemporary ministers, they seem to have been centered in the towns, largely bypassing the rural farming populations. Even within the towns, these revivals do not appear to have involved a cross section of the population. Ministers wrote that converts were usually young, most often between the ages of fifteen and twenty-five, either single or married but without children, and predominantly female. One minister estimated a proportion of three female to two male converts.[1]

According to ministers' accounts of these revivals, converts came largely from "respectable" families, usually the adolescent or young adult children of parents who had retained their ties to the church; and sent their children to Sunday School. This description of the social base of early nineteenth-century revivalism is borne out by the conversion accounts published by the evangelical press of the time. According to converts' occasional remarks about their fathers' or their own occupations, most of them were of what might be called the middle stratum of New England society: they were the children of shopkeepers or skilled artisans, occasionally the children of farmers, and rarely if at all the children of common laborers.

Probably both sources understate the involvement of poorer people in early nineteenth-century New England revivalism. Ministers were anxious to portray revivals as respectable and may have overlooked poor people who took part in them. Probably it was the better educated among the converts who sent accounts of their conversion experiences to religious journals. Certainly some of the poorer young people participated in revivals. Evangelical journals often printed accounts of revivals that swept through textile factories, and while some of the young women who worked in these factories may have been of relatively comfortable background, others must have been the daughters of poor farmers and common laborers. These revivals cannot have been entirely restricted to the comfortable middle stratum.

Even so, the tone of these revivals was set by the emerging middle class of the towns, whose desire for respectability discouraged any repetition of the raucousness of the Great Awakening. The revivals of the early nineteenth century, especially those that took place in the eastern sections of New England, were quite mild in tone. The young women and men who participated were not likely to sing or cry in the streets, to present their ministers with ultimatums, or to organize themselves into separate congregations. Occasionally, groups of young people found themselves overcome with religious feeling and unable to go on with their work or their studies. But even these demonstrations of feeling lacked the disruptive quality that had been present in many of the revivals of the Great Awakening. To some extent, the relative quietness of these later revivals reflected the influence of the clergy, who, while eager to promote conversions and to enlarge their congregations, were anxious to avoid the disorders of the past. In the last instance, however, the relative respectability of these revivals must have reflected a desire for restraint on the part of participants.[2]

In contrast to eighteenth-century patterns of conversion, in the nineteenth-century revivals men's and women's accounts of their experiences were sharply dissimilar. Among women, the desire to rebel against God's authority often became the paramount issue. Yet they feared the consequences of such desires and longed to achieve the security that submission and salvation would bring. Female conversion experiences were emotionally highly charged, and at their center was a set of internal conflicts that women and their ministers understood as issues of original sin. Men's experiences were often quite different: frequently, it was social pressure, especially from women, rather than the need to resolve internal conflicts that drove men to convert. And they either disregarded the question of original sin or gave it much less weight than they did particular sins. Men were likely to speak of conversion more perfunctorily than women and to describe the rewards of salvation in a practical way. Instead of seeing conversion as an affirmation of their worthiness, they often saw it as assurance of entrance to heaven, relief from guilt about particular sins committed in the past, and respite from the pressure put on them by religious relatives, especially women. For women, salvation also brought assurance about the future, but just as importantly it brought surcease of self-condemnation and a new self-confidence.

The typical nineteenth-century woman convert was much more concerned with rebellious desires than her ancestors, for whom this had been only one among many sinful impulses. But in spite of this shift of emphasis, the conversions of early nineteenth-century women remained consonant with orthodox Calvinism in that they focused upon the question of original sin. When men downplayed original sin, they moved away from orthodoxy. Ministers and their congregations tolerated this deviation partly because male converts were hard won at this time; in order to attract men, churches were willing to overlook some irregularities. Furthermore, though the revival ministers of this period professed orthodox Calvinism, in fact they had moved some distance themselves from the standards set by the ministers of Jonathan Edwards's generation. With the general decline of religiosity in American life, many of them were willing to take measures to encourage revivals and conversions that earlier ministers would have regarded as presumptuous, as trespassing on God's prerogatives. And with the spread of the Enlightenment among educated circles in the United States, many ministers had begun to put more emphasis on actions—both on actual sins and on the good deeds that indicated salvation—than was strictly consonant with Calvinism and less emphasis on original sin and the internal state of the convert.

This loosening of the definition of Calvinism, and of the outlines of an acceptable Calvinist conversion, made possible a greater range of conversion experiences than earlier. The masculine and feminine styles of conversion that emerged in the early part of the century reflected a growing disparity between the lives of these men and women and between the issues that concerned them. This disparity of style was intertwined with a growing conflict between the sexes, a conflict that found expression in revivalism. Women often regarded revivals, and especially the conversions of formerly irreligious men, as victories, though they were careful to point out that in scoring such triumphs they were acting only as the agents of Christ and not for themselves. In many families revivalism became a focus of conflict, in which were at stake not only divergent religious convictions but also a woman's relative power in the family, such as her right to go to a religious meeting without her husband's approval or her ability to bring him into church with her.

Men's Resistance to Calvinism

The clash in male and female attitudes toward religion was often apparent from the very beginning of a revival. Most revivals were initiated by the conversion of a young woman or a group of young women, and often the efforts of such women to spread the revival were opposed by men. In Litchfield, Connecticut, a revival began when a number of young women were struck with guilt upon preparing to go to a party, and religious concern quickly spread to other young women of the town. A group of young men decided to hold a ball in order to stop this spread of religiosity; if the young women of the town were not willing to come to their ball, they said, they would invite friends from elsewhere. "In the midst of their folly," the minister wrote, "a number of the most active of these young men were deeply impressed; relinquished their favorite object; and before the day arrived, were prepared to spend it with the people of God, in prayer and praise."[3] It was of such conversions that ministers were particularly proud.

Young men especially, according to the accounts of ministers, often ridiculed converts, refused to attend church themselves, and conspired to break up revivals in progress. Their conversions represented the victory of Christ over his opponents—and probably the presence of men in a congregation gave it a stature that women's presence could not bring.

Men who opposed revivals, and those who resisted urgings that they themselves convert, often raised theological objections to Calvinism, especially to the doctrines of human depravity and of the total dependence of human beings on the mercy of an omnipotent God. Some men were not sure whether these doctrines were false or true, but they considered them unfair; in any case, the idea that they were helpless and God all-powerful made them angry. A minister wrote of one man who

> was much opposed to the sovereignty of God and other doctrines connected with it. He did not believe them, but in case they were true, he believed they were very cruel and unreasonable. . . . He was however brought under conviction. He then saw these doctrines to be true, but hated them. . . . At length his heart became hopefully changed.[4]

Such men were likely to be attracted by the liberal forms of Protestantism—Universalism and Unitarianism—then spreading through New England, because these sects permitted a greater role in shaping one's own destiny, because they described people as basically good rather than evil, and because they made hell seem less threatening and entrance to heaven more likely. One man wrote, "For a time I strove hard to disbelieve the doctrines of the Gospel . . . particularly the doctrine of the endless, future punishment of the wicked. I listened to the arguments of the Universalists. . . . I fled for refuge to Arminianism, but all was in vain."[5] In a similar vein, a minister wrote of a man who objected especially to the statement that "God hath foreordained whatsoever comes to pass";[6] and a man who had been a Universalist, when he determined to become a Calvinist, found that he especially "remained opposed to the doctrines of the entire depravity of the carnal heart, divine sovereighty, and election."[7]

These men resisted in large part, no doubt, because they found in Calvinist doctrines a denigration of human abilities and worth that ran counter to their own view of themselves. Men who prided themselves on their work and who believed that whatever success and status they had achieved were the result of their own unaided effort and therefore well deserved were likely to be attracted to doctrines that placed more confidence in human efforts. Furthermore, men who were intent on commercial or professional success might have found the emotional intensity demanded by Calvinism disruptive. The rationality and emotional control that seemed most favorable to worldly success were more compatible with sects that stressed good behavior than with Calvinism, which demanded soul-searching and the emotional crisis of conversion.

Probably many eighteenth-century men had felt the same conflict between Calvinism and the pursuit of trade. In the early eighteenth century, trade and especially land speculation were expanding in New England and absorbing an increasing proportion of men's attention, but there was as yet no ideological alternative to Calvinism. In the nineteenth century it was possible to turn to Unitarianism or Universalism or even to attack organized religion generally. In the rural communities of eighteenth-century New England, there had been virtually no language available to explain one's discomfort with Calvinism. During the Great Awakening, men had converted in as large numbers as women, and with no special urging. Many of them had spoken with chagrin of their absorption in worldly affairs and their indifference to religion. In the nineteenth century it became possible for men to defend their absorption in worldly activities. On the secular plane, they could identify with the success stories in magazines and other popular literature. Because these stories were invariably about boys and men, not girls or women, such fantasies were available to men in a way that they were not to women, and they may have constituted one exit from an oppressively pessimistic religious tradition.

While some men may have adopted a purely secular outlook, many were not able to cut themselves off from religious concerns so easily and were therefore attracted to the more liberal alternatives to orthodox Calvinism. They could argue that the Universalists were right, that they would be saved not by God and not by faith but by their own good deeds. To some, however, this argument appeared treacherous when applied to their own lives: actions taken to promote one's worldly interests did not necessarily accrue moral or religious merit. One man wrote, upon examining his life, "I had a lively sense that in all my strivings I had no sincere regard to God, but had been activated in everything by pure selfishness."[8] Another man

reckoned up his good deeds, which he had been placing to his credit for many years; and found as he thought they were so numerous and of so good a quality that a just

God could not send him to Hell. . . . But the thought occurred to his mind, that he might have some evil deeds and he would add them up also, compare them with his good works and strike the balance. He accordingly began to reckon them up, one by one, and soon found that they were more numerous than he had ever imagined. Many things recurred to his mind of which he had not thought for years; and many others, which he had always considered innocent, appeared then to be heinous sins in the sight of God. . . . He began to see clearly that, on the ground of good works, he was gone.[9]

Nineteenth-century men who converted, as we have seen, tended to feel the sharpest guilt over particular sins, while women tended to emphasize a pervasive sense of the sinfulness of their beings. At first, men might insist upon their ability to save themselves by their deeds, but once they became convinced that their deeds were insufficient they became concerned with actual sins. They spoke of neglect of religion, drinking, gambling, "frivolous company." One man became "dissipated" and deserted his wife and children; he returned home and became religious. Few men emphasized the issue of original sin, whereas few women spoke of actual sins other than that of religious indifference. In the sample studied here, only two women spoke of more worldly sins, both mentioning frivolous behavior. For most of these women, original sin quickly became the main issue.

Nineteenth-century men were frequently either uninterested in religion or actively opposed to it and were eventually brought into the church by religious wives, daughters, or mothers. On the other hand, few women were brought to religion by any men other than ministers. Among the forty-seven male converts whose accounts have been examined in this study, sixteen mentioned the influence of religious women in their families; the rest either did not mention their families or spoke of them only in passing. None of the women mentioned the influence of men in her family. The evangelist Charles Finney wrote in his autobiography of twelve families in which one person had encouraged another to convert. In ten of these cases the wife influenced the husband, and in one a young woman influenced her parents. In the last case, a husband influenced his wife, but he had been influenced by his mother, who had prayed for his conversion.[10]

Men's opposition to Calvinist religion often involved a mixture of hostility to Calvinist doctrines, to God himself and especially his power to rule over them, and to women who became religious or urged these men to convert. In some cases a man's first response to his wife's becoming religious was to turn against her or threaten to leave her. One man wrote:

My sisters were awakened, and greatly distressed for their immoral interest. I thought them foolish to spend their time in the manner they did. My wife soon became a subject of the work. This greatly increased my opposition. . . . I used every indirect method to prevent her attendance on religious meetings. Such was the depravity of my heart that she, who, when thoughtless, was the object of my delight, was now . . . undesirable.[11]

For some men, guilt about hostility to religion was closely interwoven with guilt about opposition to their wives. A minister wrote of one instance:

A husband was so opposed to his wife's making a profession, that he was determined to forsake her if she did. But in the midst of his opposition he became convinced of his own guilt, and asked what he should do to be saved. . . . His wife directed him to the Savior. . . . The meekness of temper with which she had received his reproaches softened his resentment, and under the influence of prayer, as he expressed it, the enmity of his soul seemed to melt like wax before the fire.[12]

Such guilt was often a central issue in men's conversions. A minister told the story of a young man

who was inclined to infidelity and made light of the revival when it began, calling it delusion, enthusiasm, and priestcraft. As his wife was among the first who appeared seriously impressed, he endeavored to divert her and hinder her attention, and ridicule her out of her seriousness.[13]

This man swore that he would never attend church with his wife, but one Sunday he was persuaded to accompany his family to meeting.

As he entered the meeting house, he was first of all powerfully struck with the recollection that he had sworn never to go there again with his wife. He was greatly affected and in tears for a considerable portion of the religious exercises. . . . After a while he was relieved of his distress of mind 'and obtained a hope, that he was reconciled to God.[14]

Male Conversions

Nineteenth-century men were often reluctant converts, brought to religion either by pressure from women or by the conviction that if they were to continue in their present state they would probably go to hell. A lawyer, who had been a detached observer of a revival, went out of town one day on business:

It turned in his mind that the Bible was the best law book, the eternal rule of right between man and man. The same thought occurred frequently to his mind when going home, and when he retired for the night, but it gave him no particular alarm. When he awoke before day the same impression was running in his mind, "The Bible is the best law book." He rose, made a fire, and while he sat meditating on this impression, all at once his soul was filled with rapture. He beheld such glory and beauty in the divine character as he could not describe, and his mouth was immediately filled with praises.[15]

Another man made a calculated decision to convert because it occurred to him, when a revival began in his town, that this might be his last chance. He was thirty-six years old and aware that few people converted beyond that age.

The conversion experience of nineteenth-century men were usually briefer than women's and involved a less personal relationship to God. In the eighteenth century, both men and women might take to their beds and contemplate suicide; when they experienced salvation they might speak of "finding love for God and Christ," "trusting their souls with God." Nineteenth-century men were unlikely to feel anguish over their distance from God before they converted or to rejoice in their love for God when they did experience salvation. These men talked more about their fears of hell than about their relationship with God. When they did discuss this relationship, some were more concerned with the issues of God's power and their own than with their love for God or his for them. One man described God's power, and his own feeling of powerlessness in the face of it, in terms of property rights. He dreamed that his daughter begged him to convert; upon waking, he wrote,

I arose, and taking my garment to put on, it appeared to me that it was God's; and I trembled to think how I had used God's property. All that I turned my eyes on looked like God's things. When I opened the door and beheld the world, and the rising morning, the appearance was the same. And the view of the terrible majesty of that God, whose were the heavens, and the earth, and all this, so overwhelmed my mind, that it took away my bodily strength. I turned about and fell on my knees, for I had not strength to stand.[16]

Some men felt a closer relationship to God. A male student, for instance, wrote to his father of the revival that was taking place in his college and of his own conversion:

I sometimes felt myself powerfully and obstinately opposed to the government of God, upon the ground that He had placed me in this situation of torment, without giving me the power to extricate myself, even when on *my* part I was perfectly willing to be saved; . . . [A minister pointed out] the fatherly disinterested benevolence of God in saving sinners: when my burden seemed to drop from me, and I felt sensibly relieved. The appearance of everything was altered, and I seemed radically . . . to give up myself, both body and soul, for time and for eternity, into the hands of my Maker.[17]

Like other men, this young man emphasized his discomfort with the notion of God's omnipotence; but his ecstatic surrender to God was no different than the experience spoken of by many young women.

A few men described the same sense of pervasive sinfulness so often felt by women. Alfred Bennett, who later became a leading revival minister, wrote of his youthful conversion:

Someone meeting me one evening said, "E. B. is converted." With the sound of that word there arose in my bosom a feeling of which until that time I had remained unconscious. I could not have believed my heart was so desperately wicked. For there burst forth a spirit of enmity against God which I had no power to control. I said God is unjust, I am as good as E. B. is. . . . if God saves him and leaves me, I hate Him. I wish I could destroy Him.[18]

But it was rare for men to express such intense feelings during conversion, for them to feel such intense anger toward God or such shame about themselves. It is probably no accident that one of the few young men who had such a "feminine" conversion experience should have later become a minister: probably it was easier for men whose concerns were closer to women's than were those of most men to spend their lives in the church.

The typical male conversion experiences of this period were much more restrained than the above examples, conforming much more closely to the demand made by nineteenth-century American culture for male emotional restraint. In a letter to the evangelist Charles Finney, a wife described her husband's state:

I do not think him converted, yet I never saw a man more altered—he frequently converses with me freely upon the subject of religion—says he would weep continually if he followed the dictates of his feelings, but he thinks that it is not best, for many weep away their convictions and go down to Hell. . . . He has troubles about prayer. . . . I have often expressed my feelings about the woe which is denounced [sic] against the families that call not upon the name of God. He never answered me 'til today—today I asked him what he thought of praying in his family, he said he thought 'twas best, but he wished I would let him take his own counsel. . . . He regrets exceedingly being kept from meeting, but says he must attend to his Patients.[19]

Female Conversions

In comparison with the conversion experiences that men typically described, women were much more emotional and experienced God more intensely. Women tended to give overwhelming emphasis to this aspect of conversion, often totally neglecting other questions. All but a few women paid little if any attention to specific sins, often writing that their lives had been free of sinful behavior and that this had led them to believe that they were good Christians. When a revival began, many of these young women would be led by self-examination to conclude that they had been hypocrites: moral behavior had masked indifference to religion. One young woman wrote,

At the time of my first serious impressions I was sixteen years old, and had to that time lived a careless and stupid life, a stranger to God and Christ, and to things sacred and divine. I thought I was not very bad as I refrained from stealing, lying, swearing and other open violations of God's holy law, not considering that he looks at the heart.[20]

Some women were mainly concerned that they had neglected their religious duties and would be punished for it, but most felt real anguish over their estrangement from God. One woman wrote of the pain she felt upon discovering "the amazing distance I was at from God";[21] and another confessed, "How often I had attended upon the public worship of God, and heard as though I heard not, with little or no concern . . . even, when professedly joining with the people of God, in prayer, my heart had been far from him."[22] Another woman, who did not as yet consider herself saved, described her state in a letter to Charles Finney. "For the most part," she wrote, "I can pray with confidence, but sometimes, for a whole day together, I can only weep before God, my heart breaking with longing to behold His glory, and can scarcely open my mouth."[23]

As women examined their souls many of them discovered that beneath their former indifference to religion lay a far worse sin: hatred of God and Christ and a desire to rebel against them. A young woman wrote:

I came under conviction but still I could not forbear crying to God for mercy. I hated the Bible because it contained my condemnation. I felt that God was partial in showing mercy to others and not to me. The enmity in my heart rose against Him; and indeed I wished there were no Christ.[24]

Other women described similar feelings, one writing that she "hated God with all her heart,"[25] and another that she hated the Bible and was tempted to burn hers but refrained because she realized that even if she did "the truth would remain."[26]

Some women may have emphasized these feelings in part because ministers encouraged their expression; according to Calvinist theology, all unconverted sinners could be expected to harbor rebellion against God. These feelings were so commonly expressed during revivals that opponents of evangelical religion as well as Calvinist ministers attempted to explain them; one critic of revivals wrote that such feelings were simply a natural response to unreasonable theology.

Many persons are made to think that the reasonable anger they feel at their treatment by Calvinist ministers, the moral horror with which Calvinist doctrines strike them, are the workings of a depraved nature, "the opposition," as they are taught to call it, "of the natural heart."[27]

But the source of these rebellious feelings was deeper than either anger at Calvinist doctrines or a desire to produce the evidence of sin that a Calvinist conversion required. Women especially wrote with horror of what they found in their hearts. One young woman wrote, "I began to find, not only that I had a wicked heart, but that it was . . . filled with the most dreadful and daring opposition to God."[28] And some ministers were amazed at the depth of hostility that conversion could tap. The minister in Stockbridge, Massachusetts, recalled a young woman who had applied for membership in his church and had admitted that while under convictions "her enmity rose to such a height, that she could have consented herself to go to Hell could she but carry God with her. The human heart is and must be desperately wicked," he commented.[29]

Sometimes women's anger was directed at authorities other than religious ones. One young woman wrote in a letter to her minister.

At certain times, my heart even dared to rise in open rebellion, against the justice and government of an infinitely wise God. . . . O sir would you believe it? I even presumptuously wished the restraint of my parents was no longer binding, that I might indulge without control in all the vanity my sinful heart desired.[30]

Ministers themselves sometimes became the targets of this anger. One wrote that some converts confessed such hostility only after having been admitted to the church, but the feelings of others were so strong that while under convictions they "broke out in bitter expressions."[31]

Men only occasionally expressed anger in the course of conversion— toward religious wives who pressed them to convert, toward their ministers, or toward God. It was rare for either hostility or the consequent guilt to become overwhelming. Women, on the other hand, castigated themselves fiercely for such feelings. One woman, upon discovering the depth of her opposition to God, wrote of her "exceeding wickedness and criminality, and felt as if she was the most vile unworthy sinner on earth."[32] Another said that such "sins rose like mountains before her," and another announced, after examining her feelings, "I abhor myself."[33] A young woman of West Simsbury, Connecticut, wrote in a letter to a friend,

For a certain period, during two or three weeks, the black catalogue of the sins of my whole life appeared to be set in most dreadful order before my eyes; accompanied by a sense of being in the hands of a holy sin hating God; and solely and entirely at his disposal.[34]

Her minister, who had submitted the letter for publication, commented, "the reader will not suppose that the author of this letter was outwardly immoral. She was a person of good moral conduct. But when the law comes, it showeth even a polished soul his sins."[35]

The conflict between the desire to rebel against a hated God and the guilt caused by such feelings was for many women the central issues of conversion. Several told of having been driven almost to suicide; in the depth of convictions they felt that even hell might be better than continuing in such a state, that it might at least provide an end to the tumultuous conflicts inside them. As one woman wrote,

I felt opposed to God and holiness. My heart rose against the Bible. I could find nothing in it but what was against me, and for that reason I dreaded to read it. Although I was sensible I never could be happy with such a heart as mine, yet my aversion to holiness was so great that I rather chose annihilation. I found that instead of growing better I grew worse; that my heart was altogether vile, and that I did nothing but sin. On the evening of Wednesday, February 5, 1980 . . . I saw my heart to be completely full of pride and all manner of wickedness. . . . I entreated my maker to call me into eternity that very night. During several days a sovereign God permitted me to meet temptations too shocking to relate; but his power mercifully preserved me.''[36]

And a young woman of Torrington, Connecticut, wrote,

I longed to be spoken out of existence, for the more I learned of the divine character the more I hated it, and could not endure the thought that the Lord reigned and that all things were at His absolute disposal. Even death appeared desirable though it should make me eternally miserable.

The moment of conversion came when these feelings were overcome; God and Christ seemed no longer tyrannical but loving, and the desire to rebel was replaced by the desire to obey. The young woman of Torrington continued,

On Monday evening I felt an unusual calm in my mind for which I could not account. Opening a Bible I thought there was something in it sweet and engaging that I never saw before. . . . Christ appeared to me to be the chief among ten thousands, and altogether lovely, I rejoiced that there was so glorious a being at the head of the universe, I was sure that He would do perfectly right. I saw that God had an absolute right to do with me as He pleased. . . . I thought I would love Him if He should take me and dispose of me just as He saw fit. I desired nothing so much as to live to His glory—to serve him my whole heart.[37]

For many nineteenth-century women, conversion meant the conquest of angry, rebellious feelings and their replacement with joyful submission. But the "rebellious heart" was not so easily defeated. Especially after they came to consider themselves saved, women were likely to press others, especially men and children, into religion and to use such campaigns as vehicles for denouncing others, especially husbands. A large number of revivals were precipitated by women who met to pray for an awakening or for the conversion of particular people, often men and children in their families. A woman in western New York wrote to a relative,

> Every day we have an hour of prayer at our church . . . for females. There Christian members of all denominations meet to pour out their heart's agony for husbands and sons, for brothers and friends; it is an hour of weeping and strong supplication, and we do feel that these prayers have gone up before the throne of God—perhaps to be answered when we have entered into our rest.[38]

The minister of a congregation in Bath, Maine, wrote that "in a certain neighborhood, all the wives were persons of piety. These females were given to prayer. For this purpose they met together. Their husbands were always the subjects of prayer. Their prayers were answered. Every husband, we trust, has become a Christian indeed."[39]

These prayer campaign were most common in the more recently settled areas—western New York, northern New England—where in many towns churches were not yet established and ministers were willing to risk incendiary methods to recruit new members. Ministers of long-established churches in the older areas of Massachusetts and Connecticut discouraged such practices in their own churches and denounced their use elsewhere. They were especially critical of ministers who allowed women to pray aloud before a mixed congregation, especially if they mentioned sinners by name. According to one critic, when this was allowed "some women found themselves converted, and in the midst of a crowded assembly, and in a loud voice, began to pray for their husbands."[40]

The conflict between men and women extended to the home as well. In their accounts of revivals, ministers often told stories of men who tried to prevent their wives or daughters from attending church and who were eventually brought into the church themselves by these women. In one such story, a woman announced to her husband that she and the children intended to join the church. The husband ordered her to wait until he was ready to join as well and warned her,

> If she had any affection for him, and as she valued the peace of the family, not to go forward. . . . "No," said she, "I love you most tenderly, but I love Christ more. I

have waited for you more than twenty years, and now I shall go forward, and as to the consequences, I will leave them with Him in whom I have put my trust." The husband took his hat, and uttering some threats, left the house, as if never to return to the family again.

In these stories the husband always saw his error, and religion prevailed. In this case the husband secretly followed his wife and children to church and watched while they made their confessions and were received into the congregation. The husband was stricken with guilt, "reviewed the dreadful rebellion of his heart, and cast himself at the feet of Jesus."[41] The woman, it was stressed, always accomplished her ends without abandoning the meek, submissive posture required by the nineteenth-century code of feminine as well as Christian behavior. She never reproached the man for his irreligion or his cruel treatment of her, but her patient suffering brought him to see his behavior in a new light.

According to another story, a father forbade his daughter to attend a revival meeting and sent a spy to the meeting to see if she was there. The spy reported that she had attended, and on her return the father refused to let her enter the house. The daughter went to a neighbor's house where

the night was spent in prayer for her father. The father . . . could not sleep; his cruel conduct toward his daughter led him to see the wickedness of his heart and to cry for mercy. As soon as it was light he went to the house where he supposed that his daughter had gone. . . . "My daughter," said the father, "will you forgive me and come home and pray for me?" She accompanied him home, went into a room with her father, knelt down and prayed, and her father prayed. During these prayers the heart of the father broke. He became reconciled to God and reconciled to his daughter.[42]

These stories were part of the popular religious culture of the period, more an indication of attitudes or fantasies, especially those of women, than a record of actual events. Their significance lay in the fact that the audience of the religious journals read and enjoyed them. And, given the greater involvement of women than men in the church and with religious issues, surely this audience must have been mainly composed of women. In these stories women stayed within the limits of feminine behavior and at the same time managed to assert themselves and even impose their wills upon men, and though the stories were fiction, conflicts of this sort did take place in many nineteenth-century New England families. Opponents and supporters of evangelical religion argued about who was at fault, evangelicals supporting the women, opponents of evangelism the men. Lyman Beecher, a prominent minister and a supporter of revivalism, gave an example of "how . . . religion disturbs the families of the religious." A wife or daughter is converted and asks permission to attend revival meetings; she is forbidden. But "she feels bound by an obligation higher than man can impose, to profess Christ according to her own view, and come to his table," so she defies her husband or father and attends the meeting. On her return, Beecher wrote,

she is reproached, chided, scolded, and it may be *beaten,* by the hands of her husband or father . . . and thus having distracted and disturbed his whole house, he now sallies forth, to curse revivals of religion, and to tell how they . . . disturb and destroy domestic peace.[43]

Critics of evangelism saw these conflicts differently. A minister who opposed the revival in his town wrote that as a result of it "there are many men, who begin to doubt whether they hold that place in their houses, and in the affection and regard of their wives and daughters, which, by nature, by law and by gospel, belongs to them."[44]

Stories told by revivalist ministers often testified to the conflicts between the sexes that revivals brought close to the surface. One minister told of a woman who converted in the course of a revival meeting: "The first exhortation she gave was, as she flung herself upon the neck of her husband—an unconverted man—'O my dear husband, you *must submit,* you must submit.'"[45] And Charles Finney told of a man whose converted wife prevailed upon him to come to a revival meeting, where he experienced salvation. "I can never forget the appearance of his wife," Finney wrote, "as she sat and held his face in her hands upon her lap. There appeared in her face a holy joy that words cannot express."[46]

In these conflicts women showed the same anger and rebelliousness toward men in their families, and the same ambivalence about that anger, that they expressed toward God in the course of conversion. Religious zeal was legitimate; protesting male authority was not. Only in the name of something as deeply held and long established as orthodox religious belief could women bring themselves to challenge the supremacy of their husbands and fathers. For the same reasons, a religious challenge was more difficult for men to meet than a more direct threat would have been. But the decisive factor was the feelings of the women themselves. Resentment over their subordination to men brought vehemence to their condemnation of irreligious men, but they could not have directly repudiated that inferiority with the boldness with which they defended religion.

The Sources of Conflict between the Sexes

The divergence in world views of men and women that emerges from their conversion accounts reflects the actual divergence of their worlds. Though they lived in the same houses, men and women spent their days doing very different things, which required different outlooks—not only different but conflicting, for men's and women's values represented competing social orders. In order to succeed in the new world of commercial capitalism, men had to learn to separate morality and sentiment from self-interest, while women, in legitimizing their own domestic activity, called upon the values of the society that commercial capitalism was engaged in destroying.

Conflict between the sexes was not new in nineteenth-century New England, as eighteenth-century court records attest.[47] In the nineteenth century, however, when men and women sparred with one another they were likely to do so not merely as individuals but as representatives of antagonistic cultures. As long as women were required to be domestic and men to compete with one another in the outside world, no real resolution of this conflict was possible, for while male and female roles required one another, each was built upon the repudiation of the other's values. Domesticity, or "femininity," required that a woman have a husband who brought home the rewards of competitive labor and also that she reject the values such work entailed. The reverse was true for men: "masculinity" required having a "feminine" wife while rejecting "feminine" values.

There were practical reasons as well for the hostility between the sexes in the early nineteenth century. For a man, marriage meant taking on for life the burden of supporting other people: first a wife and then the children that the marriage produced. If the man were a storekeeper or artisan, sons might eventually be of assistance at work, but where farm boys had begun helping their fathers by the age of six or seven, urban boys spent more time

at school and often could not be of much help in their fathers' more compli-
cated tasks until a much later age. In old age a man might be supported or
cared for by his grown children, but in the nineteenth century this might be
the only time a man received economic support instead of providing it.
Nineteenth-century men married because they wanted families; because the
pressures of their lives created a need for the emotional support that marriage promised; and because, without wives, men would have had to cook
their own meals, mend their own clothes, and perform countless other vital
tasks for which they were ill prepared and which they would have regarded
as demeaning. But although nineteenth-century men had many reasons to
marry, over the course of the century they began to show their resentment of
women. Young men dreamed of going west and escaping the constraints of
what they regarded as an effeminate civilization; once married, divorce was
virtually impossible, but it was commonplace for men to leave their families
for extended periods of "travel." Male resistance to female religiosity was
part of a larger pattern of resistance to the demands that women made upon
men and to the values that women espoused.[48]

Domesticity contributed to male hostility toward women but was a
much more important factor in female hostility toward men. Foreign
travelers, reporting their observations of early nineteenth-century America,
often commented on the freedom and independence of young unmarried
women, which contrasted sharply with the constraint and resignation of
married women.[49] Young women's marriageability gave them, for a time, a
certain status and with it the self-assurance these travelers admired. But
marriageability lasted for only a limited number of years. Beyond roughly
their mid-twenties, women who had not married were on their way to
becoming spinsters, facing what promised to be a grim future. Women who
married exchanged the prestige of the courtship period for the subjection of
marriage itself. Women were drawn to Calvinism in part because the choice
that it posed between total subjugation and total damnation made sense in
the context of their experience. Calvinism helped women understand their
lives by providing a justification for the submission to male authority that
was in any case virtually unavoidable.

Another source of Calvinism's special attraction for women was the fact
that it recalled a time when family ties were stronger and men and women
less divided; an important aim of evangelical reform was to restrengthen
family ties. Women, of course, were more constrained by family ties than

men, but in the absence of alternatives they were most sharply aware of their large stake in the preservation of those ties. According to the accounts of ministers and religious journals, in family conflicts over religion it was the men who used threats of desertion as a weapon: women relied on their persuasive abilities and their claims to moral authority. In fact, wives as well as husbands deserted their families in early nineteenth—century New England. Newspapers frequently printed husbands' notices disclaiming financial responsibility for wives who had left home, and female desertion was common enough that some newspapers adopted a conventional symbol to accompany such notices: a female figure with a walking stick. But such behavior was considered disreputable, and it did not find its way into parables printed by religious journals. It is probable that women resorted to it only under dire circumstances.

Nineteenth-century conversion and revival accounts describe women who wanted more authority in their families, but not at the expense of losing their men. Evangelical religion might bring to the surface tensions that had existed among women long before the revival began, but religious literature encouraged the idea that evangelical religion would also be the means of bringing families together. Religious women probably liked to believe that this was so. The *Connecticut Evangelical Magazine* printed the following story about a revival in Harwich:

At Harwich, two or three vessels were ready to sail on a fishing voyage; it was proposed previous to their leaving the Port, that all the concerned should kneel down on the beach and go to prayer. The request being complied with, such was the power of the Holy One of Israel upon them, that when they arose they agreed unanimously for that time, to postpone their voyage and return to their families.[50]

This was the fantasy. In fact, even if upon occasion men were induced by religion to recommit themselves to their families, the special female claim to religion and the middle-class division into male and female territories could only reinforce the struggles taking place between men and women. The conventional moral and religious code that women appealed to in their struggles with men was hardly a firm basis for any improvement in their position: after the excitement of the revival was over, what was left was an ideology that endorsed subjugation to established authorities.

Conclusion

In New England at least, the revivals of the early nineteenth century did not constitute a social upheaval of anything like the magnitude of the Great Awakening. But in spite of the relative mildness of these later revivals they enabled female discontent to come to the surface in a way that the Great Awakening had not. This was partly because they were female revivals, and in them women may have gained the confidence to explore issues that in a male-dominated atmosphere they would have left dormant.

But the sharp difference between mid-eighteenth-century and early-nineteenth-century religious experience among New England women cannot be explained by appealing to the numerical edge that women had gained in the church by the later period. Their increasing domination of church membership was itself a symptom of deeper changes in women's role in the family and in society, changes that also were reflected in the transformation of women's religious experience. Nineteenth-century women brought their concerns about their roles as women to their religious experience because these issues had become newly pressing, especially for the town women of middle-stratum families who participated in these revivals in such large numbers. In order to understand these changes in women's religious experience, it is necessary to look at the context of daily life within which female evangelism took place, the transformation of women's work and family relations.

CHAPTER THREE

Domesticity and
Female Subordination

THE SHARP CONTRAST between female and male religious experiences in the early nineteenth century, and in particular the hostility toward male authority that women tended to express in their conversion accounts, reflected profound changes in the relations between the sexes. For middle-class women, the center of these changes lay in the destruction of the home economy and the creation of domesticity, which brought with it a new degree of dependence upon men.[1] These changes took place in the context of a general transformation of New England society: in the early nineteenth century a world of commerce and politics was being created, a world that was detached from the home in a way that no aspect of Puritan society had been and one from which women were excluded. The creation of this new society was accompanied by the development of a new set of values: individual achievement was held to measure individual worth, and wealth, power, and fame were taken to be measures of achievement. These new values fit the aspirations of men of the professional, entrepreneurial, and trading classes, but their women were being confined to domesticity and thus excluded from the concerns most valued in their own milieus. The dissatisfaction these women expressed indirectly through their religious experiences was rooted in shifts in middle-class value systems as well as in the actual reorganization of family life.

Throughout most of the colonial period, the church had been the most important factor, outside of the family, in shaping popular values. The decline in the power of the church, especially in the late eighteenth century, and the growing importance of education brought a gradual shift from church to school as the source of the dissemination of a popular morality. Probably this shift was experienced most sharply by the middle class, for in the early nineteenth century, public education, especially beyond the early grades, was most accessible to children of such families and often was largely shaped by what were seen as their needs. Schoolbooks, for example, were written from the perspective of this class, though with the hope that children from poorer families would be encouraged to adopt its precepts. While education was becoming a necessity for middle-class children, especially boys, religion was becoming increasingly incidental.

The New England schoolbooks of the early nineteenth century put forward a set of secular ideals that contrasted sharply with the Puritan ideology that had held sway for much of the eighteenth century. The *New England Primer,* which had taught generations of children that "In Adam's Fall / We Sinned All," had by 1800 secularized its alphabet: the couplet illustrating the letter *A* had now become "A was an Angler / And fished with a hook." Elsewhere, religion had been replaced by partriotism. *W,* which had been illustrated by the couplet, "Whales in the Sea / God's Voice Obey," had become "By Washington / Great deeds were done."[2]

The Secular Ideal: Liberty

The schoolbooks now coming into use in New England schools in place of catechisms and religious tracts were for the most part written by New Englanders, and they described New England as an exemplary region, but now for secular rather than religious reasons: New England was the cradle of liberty. The old religious ideology was replaced by a secular, patriotic one, according to which the United States was the best and freest society possible and New England was the source of those freedoms and represented their highest development.

These authors rarely defined the liberty they praised so highly, but by a free society they seemed to mean one in which there were few social restraints on the individual and one in which every man (not woman) was economically independent and had the opportunity to rise in wealth and status. In America, these authors believed, anyone who tried hard enough could make it. One author quoted Benjamin Franklin:

The way to wealth, if you desire it, is as plain as the way to the market. It depends chiefly upon two words, industry and frugality; that is, waste neither time nor money, but make the best use of both. . . . He, who gets all he can honestly, and saves all he gets (necessary expenses excepted) will certainly become *rich.*[3]

The goal might be social distinction rather than wealth alone, but the important point was that success was available to anyone who would try hard enough. Another author wrote:

It is interesting to notice how many of our worthiest and best citizens have risen to honor and usefulness by dint of their own persevering exertions. They are to be found, in great numbers, in each of the learned professions, and in every department of business; and they stand forth, bright and animating examples of what can be accomplished by resolution and effort. My friends, *you may be whatever you resolve to be. Resolution is omnipotent.* Determine that you will be something in the world, and you shall be something.[4]

These authors described America as the land not of actual economic equality but of equal opportunity. They accepted the existence of rich and poor and explained it as the consequence of differences in individual merit and exertion. They regarded poverty, in most cases, as the result of laziness and vice, and they freely expressed their contempt for the poor:

Poverty is the fruit of idleness. Idleness is the parent of vice and misery. The chief misfortunes that befall us in this life, can be traced to some vices or follies which we have committed. Were we to survey the chambers of sickness and distress, we should find them peopled with the victims of intemperance and sensuality, and with the children of vicious indolence and sloth.[5]

The only excuses for poverty, according to these authors, were ill luck and marriage. In colonial New England marriage had been an economic necessity; in the towns of the nineteenth century it was becoming an economic drain, though it continued to be necessary for other reasons. Wives bore and raised children, cooked meals, cleaned house, and performed the tasks that made a comfortable life possible and that men otherwise would have had to perform themselves. Furthermore, marriage remained the basis of social respectability. The authors of schoolbooks urged young men to marry, arguing that the financial disadvantages of family life were outweighed by its social and emotional benefits. One author described the man who shunned marriage because of the expense involved:

The selfish bachelor may shudder, when he thinks of the consequences of a family; he may imagine to himself littered rooms and injured furniture, imagine the noise and confusion, the expenses and the cares, from which he is luckily free; and pity his unfortunate neighbor, who has a half dozen squalling children to torment and impoverish him.[6]

But his wiser married neighbor

sighs over the loneliness of the wealthy bachelor. . . . He knows how to convert noise into harmony, expense into self-gratification, and trouble into amusement; and he reaps, in one day's intercourse with his family, a harvest of love and enjoyment rich enough to repay years of toil and care.[7]

In contrast to the matter-of-fact quality of earlier Puritan discussions of family life, the approach of the authors of these schoolbooks was sentimental and moralistic. Family life was no longer assumed; instead, it was held out as the basis of a respectable life, of a piece with such virtues as economy and self-restraint. The values to which these authors subscribed were those of a rising bourgeoisie in an emergent and expansive market economy; appropriately, the reward most often promised for the practice of these virtues was money. In one story, reprinted in several readers, a young man wished to marry, but, because he was too poor, the father of his intended bride refused permission. The young man found a bag of gold and, after struggling with the temptation to keep it, took it to his minister, who advertised for the owner. When no owner appeared, the young man took the money, married, bought some land, and, along with his wife, worked to turn the land into a prosperous farm. Ten years later, the owner of the money returned from foreign travels, stopped at the farm and asked if anyone knew anything about some money he had lost ten years earlier. The couple offered him the farm in recompense for his money, but the stranger was so impressed by the honesty and industry of the couple that he refused any payment. The story ended, "thus was honesty rewarded. Let those who desire the reward practice the virtue."[8]

In another story, entitled "Respect for the Sabbath Rewarded," a barber refused to work on Sundays because of his religious principles. He was the only barber in town to do so, and his business dropped off rapidly due to the ridicule of the irreligious. He was forced to work Saturday nights in order to make enough money to live on. One Saturday evening he was shaving a man who had just come into town and had come to this barber because no other barbershop was open at that hour. In the course of the conversation, the stranger identified the barber as the heir to an immense fortune, left to him by a long-lost uncle who lived in the stranger's hometown. The author of the story pointed out that had the barber not refused to work on the Sabbath he would never have received this inheritance.[9]

The authors of these books expressed respect for hard work, virtue, and achievement and an expectation that the reward would be monetary. Along with these attitudes went a contempt for the poor and a hatred of the rich; it was frequently implied that the riches of the wealthy were generally ill gotten, if not through fraud then at least through manipulation of the market rather than honest labor. In one reader, a rich man was described as "of a bearish aspect. His features were hard, and his heart was harder. You could read the interest-tables in the wrinkles of his brow . . . while averice, selfishness, and money-getting, glared from his grey, glassy eye." Such men were also likely to be cruel. In this story, the wife of a former friend came to ask the rich man for money "for her sick husband and famishing infants." The man answered that it was what her husband deserved for marrying a poor woman like herself and then proceeding to have a large number of children. The woman nearly fainted and staggered out the door.[10]

In the eyes of the authors of these schoolbooks, the wealthy were greedy, and the market itself was sinister; men would be lured by credit and become entangled in debt. One author advised readers to avoid any indirect financial dealings:

I dislike the whole matter of debt and credit—from my heart I dislike it. . . . I believe that it does more mischief than good, produces more trouble than accommodation, destroys more fortunes than it creates honestly. . . . The necessaries of life are few, and industry secures them to every man; it is the elegancies of life that empty the purse. . . . To guard against these some resolution is necessary; and the resolution, once formed, is much strengthened and guarded by the habit of paying for every article we buy, at the same time."

Boys could not afford to follow such advice literally if they hoped to succeed in business. The purpose of these books, however, was not practical guidance but moral training, not so much to convey information as to inculcate a certain personality type—rational and controlled, competitive, ambitious, and rigidly honest—and a set of attitudes—contempt or pity for poverty and the poor; desire for respectability, material achievement, and social status; and suspicion of the wealthy and fear of entanglement with them or the market they ultimately controlled. These were the values and attitudes of a class that saw opportunities for itself in an expanding economy, and they stood in sharp contrast to the Puritan ideals of a century earlier. Independence and worldly success had taken the place of pious self-abnegation and obedience to superiors; ambition had taken the place of humble acceptance of one's lot.

While the authors of these schoolbooks claimed that their message was universally American, in fact it was most appropriate for the sons of merchants, professionals, and relatively well-off artisans. Even in the relatively expansive atmosphere of early nineteenth-century New England, farm boys and the sons of poor laborers had little chance of economic success, and girls, of course, had none at all, except through marriage. And it was the middle-class children, especially the boys, who were most thoroughly exposed to this new ideology. Farm children still went to school only sporadically, and they and the children of the town poor were likely to leave school earlier than middle-class children. High school education was virtually inaccessible to the poor, for tuition was charged in most areas of New England. The education of girls was still regarded as less important than that of boys, and girls were likely to be withdrawn from school earlier than their brothers.

The main purpose of these schoolbooks, and probably of public education generally, was to train the members of a new middle class to strive for success; a secondary purpose was to convince those who could not succeed that it was their own fault. Perhaps it was necessary for schoolbooks to make these points as insistently and heavy-handedly as they did, for rural life and the family farm were not far in the past, and boys had to be torn from that less-driven culture if they were to contribute fully to the development of commercial capitalism.

The new culture of commercial capitalism, defined crudely by the schoolbooks, was widely accepted in the early nineteenth century, not only in New England but in the North as a whole. A wide spectrum of political groups and even the fledgling labor movement in the cities agreed that the opportunities for upward mobility were widespread, that wage workers could expect to become property owners and independent producers if they worked hard enough. There was broad agreement that the northern form of capitalism, "the system of free labor," was in the interest of all and vastly superior to southern slavery and the more rigid European class systems.[12] If these ideas were so widely accepted in the North as a whole in this period, they must have been virtually unquestioned in the New England towns where they were closest to the truth, where there was a broad petty bourgeoisie and as yet no real working class. The majority of men in these towns were self-employed in the early nineteenth century, and before the massive industrialization and rush of immigration, possibilities for upward mobility were substantial.[13]

One indication of the impact of this new culture in the New England towns lies in the sharp decline in male religiosity from the Great Awakening, when men and women converted in equally large numbers, to the revivals of the early nineteenth century, when men resisted religion so strongly. The desire for worldly success and the self-discipline, emotional control, and rational, calculating qualities that success required tended to draw men away from religion and made them particularly uncomfortable with evangelical religion, with its intense emotionality and its denigration of human abilities. The impact of the new values was evident in conversion experiences of even those men who did become religious. Unlike women, who were usually most concerned with the nature of their relationship with God, these men tended to regard salvation as a prize to be won, and they strove for that prize much as they strove for material rewards—with the same attention to the rules, the same emotional control, and the same clear focus on their object. There must have been men who had not achieved this level of self-control and whose conversion experiences were more like those of women; but the evangelical magazines rarely printed their stories. These accounts were printed mainly in order to induce other men to convert, and presumably the stories that fit the male stereotype most closely were seen as most likely to serve that purpose. These conversion accounts reflected in part a real change in the male middle-class personality and in part a shift in the male cultural model. But even if men internalized these new values incompletely, the change in the qualities they aspired to was dramatic.

The Exclusion of Women

The girls who attended New England schools in the early nineteenth century read the same books as their brothers and were exposed to the same ideas. They also learned that liberty and independence were the highest social values and that America was great because all its citizens had an equal opportunity to become rich and famous. Usually their books described these values as universal, ignoring the fact that they were meant only for one sex and avoiding the difficult question of race and slavery. But occasionally girls were reminded to admire the men who exhibited the qualities of independence and mobility, not to emulate them in their own behavior. Girls were told to limit their aspirations to marriage and motherhood and to cultivate the modesty and malleability appropriate to a dependent role. They were advised to quell whatever ambitions they might have. One piece, entitled "In Praise of Lady Jane Grey," applauded Lady Jane's modest refusal to become queen of England:

Her heart . . . had never opened itself to the flattering allurements of ambition; and the information of her advancement to the throne was by no means agreeable to her. She even refused to accept the crown . . . and desired to remain in that private station in which she was born.[14]

The qualities that girls were to cultivate stood in direct contradiction to the independence, ambition, and assertiveness that were elsewhere described as the glory of America. The ideal woman accepted her class position gracefully: "In polite life [her] manners are peculiarly engaging. To her superiors, she shows the utmost deference and respect; to her equals, the most modest complaisance and divinity; while every rank, experience her kindness and affability."[15] And, abandoning any personal ambition, she accommodated herself to her husband's position in society. One textbook told the story of a man who lost his fortune and was forced to move to a "humble cottage" where his wife was confronted with tasks to which she was not accustomed. Taking a walk with a friend, the husband expressed his fear that his wife might not be able to cope with poverty:

"She has been introduced into a humble dwelling; she has, for the first time, known the fatigue of domestic employments; she has, for the first time, looked around her on a home destitute of everything elegant, almost of everything convenient; and may now be sitting down, exhausted and spiritless, brooding over a prospect of future poverty."

But when the two men arrived at the cottage, the wife

came tripping forth to meet us. She was in a pretty rural dress of white; a few wild flowers were twisted in her fine hair; a fresh bloom was on her cheek; her whole countenance beamed with smiles. . . . "My dear George," cried she, "I am so glad you are home! I've set out a table under a beautiful tree behind the cottage; and I've been gathering some of the most delicious strawberries, for I know you are fond of them, and we have such excellent cream, and everything is so sweet and still here.— Oh?" said she, putting her arm within his, and looking up brightly into his face, "Oh! we shall be so happy!"[16]

There were advantages to this role: domesticity promised women seclusion from the harsh and uncertain economic world and relative comfort. But it also involved exclusion from the exploration and adventures that were open to at least some men, and in real life drudgery and isolation were more prominent than strawberries and cream. Some authors recognized this and tried to prepare girls for the realities of marriage. One schoolbook included the story of Melissa, who fell asleep and dreamed that two figures appeared before her, Dissipation and Housewifery. Dissipation offered her a dress and a ticket to a ball and promised her "a perpetual round of ever varying amusement. Like the gay butterfly, you will have no other business than to flutter from flower to flower, and spread your charms before admiring spectators." But Dissipation's pretty mask fell off, revealing "a countenance wan and ghastly with sickness, and soured by freftulness." Housewifery now stepped forward,

in a close habit of brown stuff, simply relieved with white. She wore her smooth hair under a plain cap. Her whole person was perfectly neat and clean. Her look was serious, but satisfied; and her air was staid and composed. She said, "Instead of spending your time in amusement, if you would enter my train, you must rise early, and pass the long day in a variety of employments, some of them difficult, some laborious, and all requiring exertion of mind or body. You must dress plainly; live mostly at home; and aim at being useful rather than shining. But in return, I will ensure you content, even spirits, self-approbation, and the esteem of all who thoroughly know you.[17]

For most women, the real choice was not even between dissipation and housewifery but between the relative drudgery and isolation that marriage involved and the poverty and loneliness of spinsterhood. Little girls had to be trained to be diligent housewives rather than lazy ones, but few of them had to be convinced to choose marriage rather than to aspire to male standards of independence. Probably the reason the schoolbooks devoted so little space to convincing girls that independence and mobility were not for them was that girls knew this all too well and did not need to be reminded of the obvious.

Over the same period a new genre of books began to appear, directed particularly toward teenage girls and young women, manuals in domesticity, marriage, and child care. These books were intended for what one author referred to as "the women of the middling classes," townswomen of some education and usually from professional, artisan, and trading families. The authors of these books were of similar backgrounds: ministers, educators, doctors, educated women with enough leisure to write. These books put forward, in great detail, a new definition of womanhood.

The Townswoman: Mother and Housewife

Where for the Puritans, and for the authors of late-eighteenth-century ladies' books, motherhood had been only one of a woman's tasks, nineteenth-century writers saw motherhood as the most important of a woman's responsibilities. One author announced that "the best pleasures of a woman's life are to be found in the faithful discharge of her maternal duties" and urged "every woman to undergo everything short of death or lasting disease, rather than refuse to suckle her child."[18] Others recognized that some women might find motherhood more of a burden than a pleasure and urged them to accept its restrictions:

The most anxious . . . if not the most important duty of married life, is that which is due to children. . . . To accomplish . . . these duties, a woman must be domestic. Her heart must be at home. She must not be on the look-out for excitement of any kind, but must find her pleasure as well as her occupation in the sphere which is assigned to her. St. Paul knew what was best for woman, when he advised her to be domestic.[19]

The importance of motherhood and the almost sacred nature of the mother-child relationship were themes not only of the women's guides and marriage manuals of this period but also of a closely related genre of didactic novels and collections of prose and poetry for women. In one such book an author quoted the same biblical phrase that had led the author of the Puritan tract on the "vertuous woman" some hundred years earlier to emphasize the qualities of authority and wisdom that were common to both parents. The nineteenth-century author emphasized instead the particular importance of the mother to her children, and her particular qualities of tenderness and affection.

"Her children rise up and call her blessed, her husband also, and he praiseth her." There is no fame in the world equal to this; nor is there a note in music half so delightful as the respectful language with which a grateful son or daughter perpetuates the memory of a sensible and affectionate mother. There are no ties in nature to compare with those which unite an affectionate mother to her children, when they repay tenderness with obedience and love.[20]

Such authors saw the woman's sacrifice of her own needs to the needs of others—not only children but husband as well—as the source of her special morality, the near sanctity of her role. Though she sacrificed herself for her children—nursing her babies even when it was physically difficult—she still held some authority over them. But in relation to her husband the woman was urged to adopt a posture of submission.

The separation of men's and women's spheres made it possible for apologists for domesticity, or those who simply wanted to make the best of it, to suggest that men and women held analogous degrees of power but simply exercised their authority in different realms.[21] But in fact the creation of separate spheres through the domestic organization of family life exaggerated the imbalance of power between men and women. Nineteenth-century women might have more immediate control over their children and over the running of their households than their forebears had enjoyed, but they were ultimately responsible to their husbands, in relation to whom they held few rights. Puritan women could complain to the courts of mistreatment by their husbands; especially in small towns, they could call upon community opinion. The late-eighteenth-century definition of married women as legally "dead to the law," subsumed in their husbands' personalities, significantly undercut the power of married women. In nineteenth-century New England community pressure remained a potent force, but urbanization and increased rates of mobility probably undermined it, and the widely expressed belief that family life was a private affair, not a public concern, made its operation somewhat more difficult.

Marriage guides, whether written by men or women, stressed the importance of a woman's adoption of a subservient stance in relation to her husband. First, she was to make herself totally receptive and responsive to her husband's emotional needs, sparing no effort to provide him with a refuge from the harsh outside world. John C. Abbott wrote:

What constitutes the centre of every home? Wither do our thoughts turn, when our feet are weary with wandering, and our hearts sick with disappointment? Where shall the truant and forgetful husband go for sympathy, unalloyed and without design, but to the bosom of her, who is ever ready and waiting to share in his adversity or his prosperity?[22]

According to Abbott, the wife was not only to orient herself toward her husband's desires by being "ever ready and waiting" but also to squelch her own feelings, avoiding disagreements with her husband and setting as her first priority the maintenance of smooth, harmonious family relations, whatever the cost to herself. William A. Alcott, the author of another domestic guidebook, agreed. "The balance of concession devolves upon the wife," he proclaimed. "Whether her husband concede or not, she must."[23] Alcott saw the woman's willingness to stay at home as central to this self-abnegation. He recognized that a woman might desire some life outside the home and might resent her confinement to it, but he argued that such impulses were at odds with the well-being and happiness of her family and must therefore be overcome. A woman, he wrote, "cannot discharge the duties of a wife, much less those of a mother, unless she prefers home to all other places and is only led abroad from a sense of duty, and not from choice."[24]

Daughters were urged to obey their fathers as unquestioningly as wives their husbands, both as training for marriage and because they were dependent upon their fathers as they would later be upon their husbands. In both cases, these authors claimed, women should show their gratitude for male support and protection with childlike docility and admiring love. Mrs. Louisa Tuthill wrote in a manual for girls:

It is the obedient daughter who will make the obedient wife. Obedient! How anti-quated! True; almost as old as the creation. . . . If strength and courage are given to man, he must be foremost in action and danger. If feebleness and timidity claim from him support and protection, what is due in return but love and obedience?[25]

The increased emphasis on motherhood and on female subservience reflected the economic realities of the age. Women were spending more time with their children, because, with their husbands working outside the home, they had more responsibility for child care than had their mothers and grandmothers. This sharpening of the division of labor between men and women also deepened women's dependence upon men. While ultimately women's functions of reproducing and caretaking made men's labor outside the home possible, on a daily basis it was men's support that made possible women's role in the home.

The corollary to female dependence was heightened male dominance, and the dominance was reinforced by the law. Colonial New England law had been biased against women, but it had allowed them some rights—in particular, by recognizing that women, married as well as single, were people in their own right, with interests that might be distinct from those of their husbands. These early courts, although secular institutions not officially linked to the church, had followed a legal tradition that was an amalgam of English common law and Puritan interpretation of biblical injunctions, and in this amalgam biblical injunctions predominated, at least as far as the family was concerned. On the whole, the Puritan interpretation of the Bible was more favorable to women than was the English common law that gradually took over as the influence of the church weakened. According to the English common law, which by the early nineteenth century had almost entirely replaced the older mixed tradition, once women were married they were represented legally by their husbands; they were "dead to the law." A married woman could not sue or be sued, she could not sign contracts, and any money that she inherited, earned, or brought to the marriage through a dowry was the property of her husband.[26] Such laws had been gradually incorporated into state legal codes through the eighteenth century, but they affected fewer women in the colonial economy, since few people earned money and the market was rudimentary. By the nineteenth century, with the development of towns and a growing market economy, laws excluding women from the courts and forbidding them to hold property put them at a serious disadvantage. In the second half of the century, the status of married women was improved by the passage of a series of state Married Women's Property Acts, spurred in part by pressure exerted by the feminist movement and probably in part by the dismay felt by wealthy fathers at the prospect of their daughters losing title to their inheritances through marriage—and perhaps losing them altogether through divorce or desertion. But in the first few decades of the nineteenth century, women lacked such protection.

Furthermore, the position of women in the early nineteenth century was vulnerable because the supervision of family life engaged in by Puritan courts was no longer possible. The individualist philosophy that was coming to pervade the towns and cities of New England allowed for no such intrusions into the family, now seen as the private domain of the husband and father. One minister wrote, in a nineteenth-century guidebook to family life,

Every family is a little state, an empire within itself, bound together by the most endearing emotions, and governed by its patriarchal head, with whose prerogative no power on earth has a right to interfere. Every father is the constituted head of his household. God has made him the supreme earthly legislator over his children, accountable, of course, to Himself, for the manner in which he executes his trust; but amenable to no other power, except in the most extreme cases of neglect, or abuse.[27]

In nineteenth-century America property was equated with independence and power. A property-owning male thus enjoyed largely unrestricted rights over home and family. Earlier community interest in family life was shut out, and the new domestic family was surrounded by a wall of privacy. With the spread of market ties, some change in family life was inevitable, but this particular reorganization was not. Married women, like their husbands and some of their unmarried sisters, could have gone to work outside the home; children could have been cared for in nurseries or by older relatives. It was not commerce or industrialization that kept women in their homes in the early nineteenth century, but men's power, legitimized by the deeply ingrained tradition of women's primary responsibility for home and child care. Women's domesticity enhanced men's power by undermining any possibility of genuine female equality and by placing wives in a position akin to that of possessions of men.

The Ideology of Femininity

Women's dependence was the basis for the nineteenth-century ideology of female submission. If women were to accept that subservience, it was necessary that they internalize male dominance, rather than simply obeying men out of fear of withdrawal of economic support or the sanctions of the law. In the early part of the nineteenth century, large numbers of New England women, including urban women, retained the responsibility for producing many kinds of household goods, while they lost the task that was first to be industrialized, that of producing cloth. Over the course of the century, other productive tasks gradually passed out of the household. This process was accompanied by a gradual shift in the kind of work performed by women in the home. They continued to cook and to clean and to perform the other tasks that went into the running of a household, but the time and energy that had once been spent on directly productive work were transferred to more emotional tasks: helping their children learn the social skills that would enable them to deal with a more complex society and giving their husbands the support they demanded. Mere brandishment of male power was not enough to make women accept domesticity; they needed also to be convinced of its importance.

This was the task of the guidebooks to marriage and motherhood and, more generally, of the ideology of femininity. The central elements of this ideology were, first, that children required full-time, undivided adult attention; second, that women were especially endowed to provide this care (and to create the homes that their husbands needed as well); and finally, that domesticity would shield women from the evil of the outside world and bring them status and power, mediated through their families.

The authors of nineteenth-century women's books told mothers that their babies were innocent and pure and must be shielded from the corrupting influences of the outside world. Mrs. Lydia Child wrote,

The mind of a child is not like that of a grown person, too full and too busy to observe everything; it is a vessel empty and pure—always ready to receive, and always receiving. Every look, every moment, every expression, does something toward forming the character of the little heir to immortal life. . . . [If a child comes into contact with] evil passions such as anger or other wrong feelings, evil enters into his soul, as the imperceptible atmosphere he breathes into his lungs: and the beautiful little image of God is removed farther and farther from his home in heaven.[28]

Such sentiments stand in stark contrast to the Puritan belief that children are born in sin and that it is the responsibility of parents to try to discipline and educate them out of their innate depravity. Cotton Mather had written, in a tract directed to parents,

Don't you know that your children are the Children of Death, and the *Children of Hell,* and the *Children of Wrath,* by *Nature?* You must know, Parents, that your Children are by your means Born under the dreadful Wrath of God; and if they are not *New-Born* before they *Dy,* it had been good for them, that they had never been born at all. . . . There is a *Corrupt Nature* in thy Children, which is a *Foundation* of all *Wickedness* and *Confusion.*[29]

The Puritan view had encouraged strong parental authority over children, but by portraying children as all too resistant to adult influence it had at least spared parents the worry, encouraged by the later emphasis on children's impressionability, that a child's character would be permanently distorted by some chance remark or event. The nineteenth-century view of child rearing required a great deal more effort, for according to this view not only was constant vigilance necessary to protect children from the corrupting influence of society but children, at least if they were male, had to be equipped to take part in that society. This emphasis on the child's plasticity made child rearing a difficult and important task, every aspect of which required training. Mothers were given detailed instructions by the women's guides of the period: a typical book contained chapters on how to inculcate religion in children, how to train them to be obedient, how to achieve the firmness and self-control necessary to develop their characters. Another book included such chapters as "Means of Developing the Bodily Sensations in Earliest Infancy," "Early Cultivation of the Intellect," "Management in Childhood," "Proper Amusements and Employments," and "A List of Good Books for Various Ages."[30]

Child raising was difficult, but fortunately, women were assured, they had special abilities for it, largely due to their innate warmth and morality. "The female breast is the natural soil of Christianity," wrote Abbott.[31] It was through their role as mothers that women could attain power, most importantly over their sons:

The earliest days of our statesmen, of poets, of our men of profound thought and original mind, are passed in the nursery, under constant care and superintendance of females. . . . How many a fair child has been nipped in the bud by improper treatment in early days; and how many have been brought to full perfection and beauty by the judicious care and attention of a mother.[32]

Through their sons, women could exert a powerful influence over society without leaving their homes:

Thus far the history of the world has been composed of the narrations of oppression and blood. . . . Where shall we look for the influence which shall change this scene, and fill the earth with the fruits of peace and benevolence? It is to the power of divine truth, to Christianity as taught from a mother's lips. . . . She who was first in transgression, must be yet the principal earthly agent in the restoration.[33]

In arguing that children's innocence placed them in need of undivided attention, that women's nature equipped them for the role, and that through this role women could reform society, the authors of women's books assumed a view of human nature that differed fundamentally from the Puritan conception. These ideas about human nature were in part changed by Enlightenment political ideology: increasing acceptance of the value of political equality tended to undermine Calvinist notions of deference. Even within the sphere of religion, the hold of Calvinism on New England thought was loosening in the early nineteenth century. Liberal forms of Protestantism were beginning to emerge, which substituted for the old doctrines an emphasis on human potential for good and a belief that one could play an active role in one's own salvation. Such ideas gained much ground among the churches of early-nineteenth-century New England, and in the academies and colleges most of the authors of women's guidebooks espoused the new liberalism.

These new ideas about human nature were widely attractive because they helped people, especially middle-class people, to understand their changing situation, in society generally and in the family in particular. The Puritan view, according to which human efforts were of little avail in the face of an omnipotent and incomprehensible God, had made sense to people who lived in a primitive agrarian society and who felt little control over their world. The new liberalism, which stressed human capabilities, made sense to people who were caught up in an expanding commercial system. In this situation, middle-class people might at least feel a new optimism and self-confidence, a new sense of their own power.

In other ways, the concepts of human nature that began to emerge around the turn of the century were tied to changes in roles within the family, especially changes in the role of women. The idea that children were innocent and malleable, thus needing constant supervision, helped to explain and to justify women's confinement in the home and also may, to some extent, have genuinely reflected new pressures. Child rearing may in fact have been more difficult for early-nineteenth-century middle-class women

than it had been for their predecessors. The limited options of a Puritan
farm child had been pretty much laid out at his or her birth and had relatively little to do with his or her personality development. Nineteenth-
century middle-class children, especially boys, faced a wider range of
options, within which such qualities as cleverness and perseverence might in
fact make a difference. Furthermore, social life had become more complex:
life in a commercial, industrializing town was doubtless more complex and
difficult than life on the farm had been. It may have been necessary to watch
children more closely in these new circumstances, and the process of training
them to take part in this new world may have been more difficult than the
task of raising children to participate in the life of a farm community had
been.

Women of the early-nineteenth-century New England towns, and, for
that matter, nineteenth-century urban American women generally, had little
choice but to accept domesticity. Domesticity went with marriage, and the
alternatives to marriage involved greater hardships than were entitled in
domestic isolation. In the early nineteenth century there was little overt
female protest against domesticity: women who spoke of it were likely to
defend it. A large number of marriage manuals were written by women, and
Catharine Beecher made a career of formulating and promulgating an
ideology of domesticity, arguing that women should identify themselves with
the home and that identification should lead them to a larger role in public
affairs. Neither the female authors of marriage manuals nor Catharine
Beecher can be dismissed as the victims of false consciousness. In a large historical perspective, domesticity represented a weakening of women's power
in relation to men, but in an immediate sense, it represented the best of all
available alternatives; and by providing women with a role that was clearly
defined and widely venerated, it offered them an arena for self-development
and a base from which to press their claims. Given that no one in the early
nineteenth century believed women would enter the world of commerce and
industry on equal terms with men, it seemed to many women best not to
enter at all. At least in an immediate sense it was in women's interest to
play as large a part as possible in defining the domestic role, in establishing
the content of the ideology of domesticity.

Marriage manuals tried to demonstrate that domesticity augmented
women's power, that through devoting themeselves to their husbands and
children women would find their own positions enhanced. It was argued
that, even though work in the home seemed trivial in comparison with men's

work outside the home, women's work in fact held families together and was therefore the basis of society itself. These manuals insisted that women were secluded from outside society because they might be tainted by contact with it, that they were superior to that world and to the men who inhabited it. And they claimed that the seclusion that preserved women's purity would bring them power, that it was women's seeming powerlessness, their self-sacrifice, that made their superiority unshakable. The authors of women's guides spoke rapturously of this subtle but invincible female power:

> Were each American female but faithful to her God, her family, and her country, then would a mighty, sanctified influence go forth, through the wide extents of our beloved land, diffusing moral health and vigor. . . . A spirit of insubordination and rebellion to lawful authority pervades our land—and where are these foes to be checked, if not at the fountain head, in the nursery? Oh! If every American mother had but labored faithfully in that sanctified enclosure . . . then soul submission to constituted authority, as well as to will of God, have been far more prevalent in our land.[34]

Such promises of spiritual and moral power, contingent only upon devoting oneself to one's family, must have been very appealing to women whose mothers and grandmothers had worked so hard in frontier settlements, had carried half the burden of running a farm without earning corresponding status or power, and must often have wished that they had more time for undivided attention to their children and relaxation with their husbands. The new ideology of femininity promised them all of this, and power besides. And through their acceptance of domesticity, these women probably did acquire a certain dubious power. To the extent that they did come to hold sway over family life, men must have felt that women had the power to exclude them from or allow them into the realm of emotional ties and warmth. And to the extent that both men and women accepted the idea that women had special access to the realms of religion and morality, women must have acquired a particular kind of authority within their families, particular confidence in making judgments within these areas.

The Price of Femininity

Ultimately, the ideology of femininity was false: women paid a price for domesticity, and a heavy one. The loss of self that domestic dependence brought with it was evident, for instance, in the rigid and antisexual moral code that women were now expected to adhere to. Women were now told to hold their own sexuality suspect:

There is a species of love, if it deserves the name, which declines soon after marriage, and it is no matter if it does. . . . There can be no objection to external love, where it is a mere accompaniment to that which is internal. What I object to, is making too much of it; or giving it a place in our hearts which is disproportional to its real value. Our affections should rather be based chiefly on sweetness of temper, intelligence, and moral excellency.[35]

The idea that sexuality was evil was a tenet of Victorian thought, applicable to men as well as women; but few people expected men to take such ideas very seriously, while women were expected to renounce sexual desire utterly. Probably this double standard rested in part on a sense that a concern with one's own satisfaction was compatible with the role of men in society but not with the selflessness required of the mother and the submission required of the wife. The price of domestic comfort, therefore, was a loss of self-assertion, in sexual as well as in economic and social life.

Dependency and powerlessness also had a physical cost: by the middle of the nineteenth century, vague, often undiagnosable illnesses were becoming widespread among the middle-class women of the northeastern towns. Women complained of headaches that would not go away, internal pains, weakness, paralysis.[36] Venereal disease may have been responsible for some of these symptoms: prostitution was spreading rapidly in this period, especially in the cities, and men who visited prostitutes often contracted diseases which they then gave to their wives. But venereal disease does not explain the particular physical frailty of middle-class women in this period. It seems likely that the balance of women's illnesses were directly related to their dependency. The tightly bound corsets that made women attractive to men, according to the standards of the age, often dislocated internal organs over many years of use; a woman's duties in her home might have prevented her from getting enough fresh air.[37] Some illnesses were psychological; hysteria, for example, sent women to their beds, secluded in darkened rooms. Such illnesses allowed women to give up their domestic tasks, at least temporarily, without stepping beyond the bounds of the female role; hysteria could be simultaneously an exaggeration of the female role and a veiled protest against it.[38] It was also, however, an invitation to the reassertion of male dominance. Some husbands may have felt helpless in the face of their wives' hysteria, but the prescribed cures—bed rest, abstinence from work, especially intellectual work, and unquestioning obedience to the doctors' orders—reinforced these women's sense of childlike dependency.[39]

Conclusion

In religious conversion as in illness, women played out the cycle of rebellion and submission, in their rebellion never going any great distance beyond the bounds of acceptable behavior, and in their ultimate submission to God confirming their adherence to the female role. The center of conversion, for these women, was accommodation to the inevitable—male dominance. If to challenge God was hopeless and defeat inevitable, acquiescence must follow. The same held true when women carried rebellion into their families after conversion, by going to religious meetings against the orders of their husbands or fathers or by denouncing their men for irreligion. Male authority was challenged, but only in the name of obedience to a higher male authority, that of God and Christ. The traditional values that women appealed to through religion evoked a time when women had held a place in society they now had lost. Women's piety and religious activity in the first half of the nineteenth century helped to create the networks and give women the experience that made possible the flourishing of women's reform organizations in the latter part of the century. This religiosity simultaneously gave encouragement to two contradictory impulses: deference and obedience to superior authority and the need to take action on behalf of cherished values.

CHAPTER FOUR

The Woman's Crusade
and Home Protection

AFTER 1840 the religious revivalism of the past four decades abated. Though sporadic revivals continued to take place in the 1840s and 1850s, evangelical religion was gradually superseded by more secularly oriented movements. Of these the temperance movement was the largest and, having originated in the churches, the most closely linked to the evangelical tradition. The temperance movement in the latter part of the century was made up primarily of the same kind of people as those that had shaped evangelical religion people of the same class and ethnic background, Congregationalists or their descendants. Unlike evangelism, temperance was a movement of social reform, but it was religiously and morally inspired social reform and had its base in the Protestant churches.

For women, the temperance movement provided another kind of continuity in that it became an arena in which old concerns, rooted in the relations between men and women, could be expressed in a new and more socially effective way. The antagonism toward men and toward masculine values that had led evangelical women to associate femaleness with piety was now translated into the secular terms of temperance.

The temperance movement began, in the early nineteenth century, as a network of organizations made up of Protestant men, men who were largely members of Congregationalist churches and of the families that liked to consider themselves "respectable." Women were at first by and large excluded from formal membership in these organizations. But women, especially middle-class Protestant women, were attracted to the issue of temperance. As temperance literature pointed out, women were often the victims of men's drinking. Beyond this, the question of temperance raised a range of issues touching on social values and family life. In the decades after 1840 women were drawn to the movement in larger and larger numbers. Limited involvement in male-dominated temperance associations and spontaneous attacks on saloons in scattered towns in New England and the Midwest culminated in the upsurge that was called the Woman's Crusade, a mass female assault on the saloons of Ohio and surrounding areas in 1873 and 1874. Out of the Woman's Crusade came the Woman's Christian Temperance Union, which would become the leading temperance organization and the largest organization of women in the United States up to that time.

In the late nineteenth century, the temperance movement came under female leadership and was transformed into what was largely a female drive against the intemperance and irresponsibility of men, a campaign against the masculine culture that these women saw as supporting such irresponsibility. Through this process, the women's culture that had begun to emerge through evangelical Christianity and the sexual antagonism around which that culture revolved were politicized. The temperance movement provided the basis for a demand for public recognition of women's values and for action by society, particularly the state, in defense of these values and the family life in which they were embedded. As women's culture became politicized, it turned a sharp edge not only against men but also against an immigrant working-class culture that these middle-class women regarded as epitomizing a vulgar masculinity. Evangelical Christianity had emerged in an America in which the working class had been neither numerically large nor experienced as a major threat by other classes. To the extent that women of this movement had developed a particular consciousness, it had been defined in conflict with the irreligious (men) of their own culture; issues of class, when raised, were posed in terms of the difference between aristocratic and middle-class ways of life. By the late nineteenth century, a culturally distinct immigrant working class was coming to be a significant factor in American social life, a factor experienced by many middle-class people as threatening. The outlook of temperance women was shaped by class as well as sexual antagonism.

It was not until the early nineteenth century that widespread concern about drinking appeared in the United States. In the colonial period alcohol was not regarded as an evil: it was one of God's gifts, to be enjoyed, like any other, in moderation.[1] Cotton Mather regarded alcohol as dangerous and preached against it, but on this issue and others, such as sex, Mather's views were considerably stricter than those of the majority of Puritan ministers.[2] Edward Taylor, Puritan minister and poet, used the image of beer spurting out of barrels as a metaphor of God's overflowing love, and women as well as men drank as a part of everyday life. Drinking took place at home, at community celebrations of all kinds, and in taverns, and Puritan ministers do not seem to have seen anything wrong with it as long as it did not lead to drunkenness. And even drunkenness was regarded with more indulgence than in later generations; the Puritans saw it as a sin of excess but not as the root cause of antisocial behavior or the source of all social problems.

Alcohol was important to the colonial economies, especially to New England's economy, which relied substantially on the importation of molasses and the production of rum. Though there are no statistics on alcohol consumption before the first census in 1790, it seems likely that substantial amounts of alcohol were consumed annually in New England throughout the colonial period. It also seems probable that the consumption of alcohol increased in the late eighteenth century, in response to the lifting of restrictions on navigation after the Revolution and the readier availability of imported alcohol. Advertisements in New England newspapers around the turn of the nineteenth century suggest that stores throughout the country were overflowing with liquor of various kinds, most of it from abroad. Whatever the trend in alcohol consumption before 1790, from 1790 to 1830 consumption rose sharply, from 5.8 gallons per adult per year in 1790 to 7.1 gallons per adult per year in 1830.[3]

The Origins of the Temperance Movement

In the late eighteenth and early nineteenth centuries, physicians, and especially ministers, began to speak out against alcohol, partly in response to the actual increase in drinking that was taking place and partly because their views reflected the moralism of those who were taking it upon themselves to guide the behavior of the emerging middle class. In 1785, for example, Dr. Benjamin Rush published a widely circulated pamphlet denouncing intemperance.[4] And in the first decade of the nineteenth century, temperance societies were formed in a number of New England towns, especially in Massachusetts, usually through the efforts of local ministers. In 1812 the Massachusetts Society for the Suppression of Intemperance was formed at the initiative of the Congregational church, and in 1826, representatives of the leading Protestant denominations formed the American Temperance

Society. These early organizations were staid and respectable; rather than missionary efforts, they were societies of the already temperate, designed primarily to help male church members stay away from alcohol. But the temperance movement quickly began to expand. In the late twenties and early thirties temperance societies were formed outside the churches, though they remained highly religious. Such organizations as the New York State Temperance Society grew rapidly, probably reaching beyond formal church members for support.[5]

Early temperance societies, whether located inside or outside the Protestant churches, excluded women or relegated them firmly to a subsidiary role. Temperance leaders told women that their primary role in the temperance movement was to keep alcohol out of their homes by training their sons not to drink and discouraging their husbands from drinking. Scattered female temperance societies existed, largely devoted to encouraging women's temperance efforts in their own homes and immediate circles. In an address before one such society, Dr. George Packard admitted in passing that some women drank but said that such a thing, fortunately, was rare. Women's main interest in temperance, he argued, arose from the fact that they were "obliged to suffer so much from the intemperance of those with whom they are connected in life. . . . Consider for a minute," he said, "the suffering and anguish endured by mothers in consequence of the dissipation and intemperance of sons." Packard urged the women to promote temperance by their own example and the examples of their homes, to make charitable visits to drunkards' homes, and, if single, to refuse to marry drinking men.[6]

In 1840 the social base of the temperance movement was greatly expanded by the formation of the Washington Society, the first major temperance society to be formally independent of the church and the first to attempt the reformation of drunkards on a large scale. The movement was inaugurated by six men who were in the habit of meeting in a Baltimore tavern. One evening, the men discussed an advertisement for a temperance meeting and, out of curiosity, sent one of their number to investigate. His report led the six men to draw up a joint pledge of abstinence. They transferred their gatherings from the tavern to the shop of one of their number and opened their meetings to men who wished to renounce alcohol. Calling themselves the Washington Society, they encouraged the formation of other groups like their own. The society spread rapidly through the cities and towns of the Northeast, and its meetings, where converts recounted the evils of drink and testified to the improvement that sobriety had brought to their lives, had much of the atmosphere of religious revivals. Leaders of the older, more exclusive, and more restrained temperance societies objected to opening the temperance movement to drunkards, arguing that backsliders brought disgrace to the movement generally. Such recruitment, the older leaders argued, was bringing lower-class men into a movement that had until this point been made up of the "respectable."[7]

The organization of the Washington Society marked a further popularization of temperance and eventually led to the greater inclusion of women in the movement; as part of their effort to broaden the movement, the Washingtonians established a women's auxiliary, the Martha Washington Society. The Washington Society lacked solid organization and declined quickly, but in its short life it had greatly enlarged the temperance movement. The societies that replaced the Washingtonians inherited their concern for expansion and also tended to include women in subsidiary organizations. The Sons of Temperance, through the 1840s and 1850s the leading American temperance organization, established an auxiliary for women, the Daughters of Temperance.

Amid the proliferation of reforms in the 1850s, causes tended to converge; in 1848 the first women's rights society was formed, and for a short period women's rights and women's temperance became intertwined. Elizabeth Cady Stanton and several other feminists put out a newspaper, *The Lily,* which for a time was primarily concerned with temperance. Feminists participated in the formation of a women's temperance society in New York and joined the Daughters of Temperance. At a national convention of the Sons of Temperance in 1852, however, the women were not allowed to speak, and male opposition to the full participation of women in the movement persuaded the feminists to transfer their support to the women's rights movement itself.[8] With the approach of the Civil War and increasing public concern over mounting sectional conflict, interest in temperance temporarily declined.

Though the men who dominated the temperance organizations placed obstacles in the way of women's full participation, women found their own ways of attacking liquor. From at least the 1830s on, in the New England states and especially the "New England belt" of settlement through the Midwest, there were sporadic, spontaneously organized women's attacks on saloons. Dio Lewis, a circuit lecturer on women's health who helped to galvanize the largest and most dramatic of such attacks, the Woman's Crusade of 1873–74 recalled a number of similar incidents in the decades preceding the crusade. It was a campaign of this sort organized by Lewis's mother when he was a small boy that had led to his interest in temperance. He recalled,

> There was trouble at our house when I was a small boy. My father had forgotten everything but drink. There were five of us small people. Our mother, with her own hands, provided for all. She earned and cooked our food, cut and made our clothes, in brief, was father, mother, general provider, cook, housekeeper, and nurse. In addition to all this she was the victim of abuse and violence. Often she would cry in the presence of her children.[9]

In the early 1830s, Mrs. Lewis persuaded a group of women in Clarkesville, New York, to confront the liquor dealers of the town. Bibles and hymnbooks in hand, they visited the saloonkeepers and prevailed upon them to cease selling liquor.

Lewis reported having heard of a similar effort in another New York town in the early 1850s, and in the late fifties and early sixties he played a role in persuading the women of Dixon, Illinois, Battle Creek, Michigan, Natick, Massachusetts, and Manchester, New Hampshire, to mount such campaigns.[10] Mother Stewart, later a leader of the Woman's Crusade, reported a similar incident in Greenfield, Ohio:

> In 1865, a very great excitement was caused by the murder of a worthy young man as he was quietly passing a saloon on the street; a shot aimed at some party in the saloon found a lodgement in the young man in the street, with fatal results. The victim was the son and only support of an aged and feeble widow. There was no law to reach the case, but a large number of the respectable ladies of the town, after some secret counsels, accompanied by the bereaved mother, proceeded to the saloon and with axes and other weapons knocked in the heads of barrels and casks, and demolished bottles and fixtures.[11]

In 1869 an Ohio woman who had participated in such an assault described it in a letter to the *New York Tribune*. A group of women in Perrysville, Ohio, had opposed the opening of a saloon in their town, and when the prospective saloonkeeper refused to sell out to them, the women destroyed his supplies of liquor. The letter to the *Tribune* concluded:

The people in this part of Ohio honestly think that the next war in this country will be between women and whiskey; and though there may not be much blood shed, you may rest assured rum will flow freely in the gutter. As the women here have taken the matter in hand once before, we claim to have fought the Bunker Hill of the new Revolution.[12]

The Woman's Crusade against Whiskey

In December of 1873 a talk by Dio Lewis at the Presbyterian church in Hillsboro, Ohio, instigated the Woman's Crusade that seized Ohio for several months, spread into other states, and succeeded in temporarily lowering the sale of alcohol quite dramatically. Lewis gave his usual temperance talk in which he described his mother's campaign against the saloons of Clarkesville and urged the women of Hillsboro to follow her example. At the conclusion of the lecture, a women's committee was formed to direct such a campaign, and eighty women met the next morning in the church, drew up temperance pledges to be presented to the liquor dealers of the town, and, after prayers and a hymn, set out in double file to confront the enemy.[13]

One saloonkeeper signed; others refused. While the Hillsboro women continued their efforts, marching in double file out of the church every morning, Lewis proceeded to the nearby town of Washington Court House, where he included in his lecture a description of the efforts of the Hillsboro women. The women to Washington Court House followed the Hillsboro women in taking up Lewis's proposal and in addition received active support from the temperance men of the town. As the women marched through the streets, their male supporters prayed in the church, ringing the church bells to encourage the women and, presumably, to help intimidate the saloonkeepers. Perhaps as a result of such audible male support, the women's efforts met with success in this case. Within a week they had closed down all of the town's eleven saloons. The victorious women then went to the aid of the Hillsboro women and, with the Hillsboro temperance men copying the tactics of prayer meetings and bell ringing, the combined group visited one saloonkeeper after another and this time persuaded more of them to close down.

The crusade now spread to surrounding towns. Where the crusaders were unable immediately to persuade a saloonkeeper to sign the pledge, their first recourse was to occupy the offender's saloon, entering as soon as it opened and staying until it closed, singing and praying and often taking down the names of any men with the courage to enter and drink. The first female sit-ins in American history, perhaps the first sit-ins of any variety, these demonstrations were enormously successful. The women embarrassed the saloonkeepers and their customers and usually destroyed the saloon's business for at least the duration of the demonstration. In some small towns, social circles were small enough that saloon customers and crusaders might easily recognize one another. For instance, a young man who had been present at one of the Hillsboro saloon visits described it to a reporter for a Cincinnati paper:

He and half a dozen others, who had been out of town, and did not know what was going on, had ranged themselves in the familiar semicircle before the bar and had their drinks ready and cigars prepared for the match, when the rustle of women's wear attracted their attention, and looking up they saw what they thought a crowd of a thousand ladies entering. One youth saw among them his mother and sister, another had two counsins in the invading host, and a still more unfortunate recognized his intended mother-in-law![14]

Fortunately for the young men, the women began to sing, and this diversion allowed them to escape by the back door.

While some saloonkeepers signed the pledge and accepted the women's help in setting themselves up in other businesses, others fought back. In the winter months some saloonkeepers ceased heating their saloons once the women's visits began; one flooded his saloon with water so as to bring the temperature down further.[15] One saloonkeeper persuaded a group of crusaders to leave by announcing that it was time for his bath and beginning to undress. Another, Charles Van Pelt, resisted the women so fiercely that he won a reputation among the crusaders as "the wickedest man in Ohio." When he heard that he was about to receive a visit from the crusaders, he swore that the prayers of all the women in town would never move him and that if the women came to his saloon he would baptize them with beer. When they came and began praying that the Lord would baptize him with the Holy Spirit, he threw a bucket of dirty water on them, saying, "I'll baptize you." When the water failed to achieve its purpose, he followed it with beer. When the women returned the next morning, they found Van Pelt flourishing a bloody ax. At this point male temperance supporters intervened; Van Pelt was temporarily jailed for violations of the law governing the operation of saloons.[16]

Especially in cases like Van Pelt's, the ultimate surrender of the saloon-keeper, if it came, was a cause for celebration. The recalcitrant saloonkeeper would formally "surrender" to the women, often in the presence of a large crowd; barrels of liquor would be rolled out of the saloon, and the saloon-keeper or the women or both would proceed to split them open, allowing the liquor to flow into the street. After his initial fierce resistance, Van Pelt began to feel the financial pinch from loss of business, and it seems to have occurred to him that becoming a hero of the temperance movement might offer some opportunities. When he made it known that he was ready to sur-render, all the church bells in town rang, and a large crowd gathered in front of his saloon. The women began to sing, and Van Pelt and several ministers rolled out the barrels. Van Pelt requested that the men in the crowd, with the exception of the ministers, leave; as this was the work of the women, he said, he wished to surrender to them. When the men left, Van Pelt gave a speech in which he said that the women had awakened his conscience and then began to split open the barrels of liquor. For a short time, he became a lecturer on the temperance circuit; large crowds came to hear from his own lips how "the wickedest man in Ohio" had been converted by the women.[17]

In the course of the crusades both sides occasionally resorted to the law. Partly as a result of previous temperance activity, Ohio law, while it per-mitted saloons, placed a number of restrictions on their operation. The sale of alcohol to be drunk off the premises was forbidden; its sale to minors, without the written permission of parent or guardian, was forbidden; and its sale to anyone who was drunk or in the habit of getting drunk was illegal. In the latter case, an amendment enabled relatives to sue those who sold alcohol to intoxicated persons. Since these laws were widely ignored, stub-born saloonkeepers who refused to close down in response to crusade pressure might find themselves in court, charged with one violation or another. At times saloonkeepers took crusaders to court, claiming that they were running legitimate businesses, that the women were trespassing, and that their intervention constituted an illegal nuisance. Some saloonkeepers persuaded judges to enjoin the crusaders from entering their saloons, in which case the women would move the demonstration from the saloon itself to the sidewalk outside, where they continued praying and singing and taking down the names of men who entered the saloon. In one such instance, the women set up a "tabernacle" on the sidewalk, complete with a locomotive headlight, which was kept trained on the saloon door to enable the women to identify those who entered after nightfall.[18]

For both sides there were disadvantages to legal action; it tended to slow down the process rather than to resolve the issue, which was fundamentally one of public attitude toward alcohol, not of implementation of the limited existing law. Unless a saloonkeeper could obtain an immediate injunction against the women, his business could be badly damaged while his case went through the courts. Even if he eventually won the case, his victory was not likely to do him much good if the women had succeeded in creating an antialcohol consensus in the town. Nor was the law a very powerful weapon for the women. Saloons were legal enterprises, and all the women could charge saloonkeepers with was running their businesses improperly. A judgment favoring the women might result in a fine or at most a jail sentence but not in the closing of the saloon.

The crusades were most successful in the relatively small towns where they originated, less successful in larger towns and cities. The crusaders themselves explained this by pointing out that public opinion operated most strongly in small communities where most people knew each other and that in the larger towns it was harder to organize the women. One sympathetic observer of the crusades wrote of an attempt in Xenia, Ohio:

This was the first trial in a city of more than eight thousand people; and it seems to show that the difficulties in every large city will be great. . . . The greatest difficulty is with the ladies themselves, and their tendency not to unite. In a small place all respectable ladies are in one social order; church and society blend insensibly, and it is comparatively easy to unite the good women for any good object. But in a city there are scores of cliques, circles, and social strata. Eminently respectable people in one circle do not know equally respectable people in another. . . . All true women shrink from publicity or open manifestation of the emotions, for obvious reasons those in a city much more than those in the country, who are known to all they are likely to meet.[19]

Another difficulty lay in the fact that Ohio's German population was concentrated in the larger towns and cities; where German communities were strong, they were better able to confront the crusaders. Especially in Ohio, and also to some extent in the surrounding states, the issue of alcohol was closely tied to tensions between the Anglo-Saxon and German immigrant communities. The culture that German immigrants brought with them was seen by some as strange and threatening; and Germans drank.

Middle-class Anglo-Saxon women's fears about alcohol provided the impetus for the first crusades, but as the movement spread to the larger towns and cities those fears were entangled with distrust of the immigrant, and the crusades themselves were enmeshed in class and ethic conflict. Crusaders spoke contemptuously, of German saloonkeepers and their German clients, and the Germans responded to the crusades as an attack on their culture. There were German saloonkeepers in the smaller towns, but they served a largely Anglo-Saxon clientele and could not afford to disregard the crusaders. In the larger towns and cities, there were many saloons that served as focuses of German community life. The owners of such establishments were not likely to undergo changes of conscience upon hearing the crusaders' arguments.

In a number of towns and cities, the actions of the crusaders led to riots or near riots. In Dayton, groups of crusaders were followed about their rounds by crowds of hecklers who threw bits of food at them; at every saloon visited by crusaders, free drinks were handed out to the crowd. On several occasions riots were narrowly averted. After nearly a month of such activity, the police commissioner forbade continuation of the women's visits, and the crusade came to an end. In Cleveland, a band of crusaders was chased by a mob; two women were injured, and the crusaders were forced to hide in a store until rescued by police.[20] In Cincinnati, a group of crusaders on their way to a prayer meeting met with an anticrusade demonstration: butchers with their sleeves rolled up and their butcher knives in their hands, men brandishing pistols. Here again, the mayor forbade the women to continue holding street meetings.[21] In Chicago, saloonkeepers made money from public hostility to the crusades. They invited crusaders to their saloons and posted notices that a prayer meeting was to be held. Large, thirsty crowds would gather to drink while the women prayed. One saloonkeeper even hired three women to impersonate crusaders and advertised that there would be two prayer meetings a week at his saloon.[22]

In the spring of 1874, temperance became an issue in a series of local elections throughout Ohio. In town after town, temperance slates, mostly Republican, ran and were defeated. In the fall state elections, the Republicans put forward a resolution "against intemperance and its causes," while the Democrats, whose base was in the cities and among the immigrant population, favored an amendment to the state constitution that would permit the legislature to enact laws licensing saloons, thus giving them official recognition as legitimate businesses. The Republicans were defected, and an important element in the defeat was opposition to temperance. In the wake of riots and unfavorable elections, the crusades died out in the summer and fall of 1874.

Over the course of a few months, the Women's Crusade had spread to 130 towns, villages, and cities in Ohio, 36 in Michigan, 34 in Indiana, and smaller numbers of towns in seventeen other states. By April of 1874 more than a thousand saloons had been at least temporarily closed. Estimates were made that during the crusade beer production in the state had decreased by a third.[23] Much of this decline was a result of the economic depression of the same year, but the impact of the crusades was also probably significant. However, the effects of the crusades on the liquor business were not lasting. Within a year most of the saloons closed by the crusade had reopened, and the consumption of alcohol had again risen. In the long run, the most important effect of the crusades was not on the saloons but on the women who participated in them. Frances Willard, later president of the Woman's Christian Temperance Union, wrote of the Woman's Crusade:

Perhaps the most significant outcome of this movement was the knowledge of their own power gained by the conservative women of the Churches. They had never even seen a "woman's rights convention," and had been held aloof from the "suffragists" by fears as to their orthodoxy; but now there were women prominent in all Church cares and duties eager to clasp hands for a more aggressive work than such women had ever before dreamed of undertaking.[24]

Alcohol and the Family

The crusaders and their sympathizers saw temperance as being, in important ways, a women's issue. Though they occasionally admitted that there were some unfortunate cases of drinking women, they believed that for the most part it was men who drank and women who suffered from men's drinking. They believed that since women had a special stake in temperance they could be mobilized more easily than men in the fight against alcohol. One temperance advocate, for instance, wrote,

There are two thousand rum holes spreading death and disease through all ranks of American society. . . . From half a million women a wail of anguish is wafted over an otherwise happy land; and over the graves of forty thousand drunkards, annually, goes up the mourning cry of the widow and orphan. The chief evils of the traffic in ardent spirits have fallen on women; and it is eminently fitting that women should inaugurate the work for its destruction.[25]

Though those who made this argument were undoubtedly right that women drank considerably less than men, especially in the Anglo-Saxon middle class from which the crusaders were drawn, this was not a sufficient explanation for these women's interest in temperance. "All ranks of American society" were not in fact equally prone to drinking, and in the "respectable" middle-class families of the crusaders men probably drank considerably less than the average and visited saloons less often than men of poorer and especially immigrant families.

Accounts of the Woman's Crusade make it clear that the class background of the crusaders tended to be at least middle class. One observer described a crusade prayer meeting as follows:

Turning the corner on last Saturday afternoon, I came unexpectedly upon fifty women kneeling on the pavement and stone steps before [a certain saloon]. A daughter of a former governor of Ohio was leading in prayer. Surrounding her were the mothers, wives and daughters of former Congressmen and legislators, of our lawyers, physicians, bankers, ministers, teachers, business men of all kinds.[26]

Even taking into account the fact that a supporter of the crusade might exaggerate the role of socially prominent women in the movement, it is clear from this and other descriptions that there were few crusaders from the poor and immigrant families in which men drank most heavily.

The Crusaders regarded saloons as the domain of lower-class men, a domain that was far removed from their own "respectable" world but one that they feared men of their own families might occasionally frequent. An observer wrote of the Hillsboro crusaders:

The thought of going into the low part of town and entering one of those vile dens which respectable people abhorred at a distance; of kneeling in sawdust and filth, and pleading with bloated and beery saloon-keepers, was overwhelming to their finer sensibilities and shocking to their modesty. . . . But, again, they thought of the drunkards that were reeling home from the saloon every night—perhaps into their families—and of the temptations that were lying in wait for their children in the future. Their misgivings left them.[27]

Some of the women who participated in the crusade had confronted serious problems connected with alcohol in their own homes, but such women were rare enough that crusade accounts made special mention of them. An observer of the celebration at the surrender of a saloonkeeper in Xenia, Ohio, wrote as follows:

Of the women around, some were singing, some laughing, and some alternately singing and returning thanks. One elderly lady in the edge of the crowd was almost in hysterics, but still shouting in a hoarse whisper such as one often hears at camp meeting: "Bless the Lord! O-o-o, bless the Lord." She had the appearance of a lady in good circumstances, and a citizen informed me that she is ordinarily one of the quietest, most placid of women. One of her sons died of intemperance, and another is much addicted to liquor.[28]

At another celebration of a saloonkeeper's surrender, several women who had themselves suffered because of alcohol were given the honor of breaking open the casks. Axes were placed in their hands, and the crowd cheered as the alcohol spurted forth.[29] Clearly there were crusaders who were themselves directly victimized by men's drinking, but they were in the minority. Most of the crusaders were not among the "million women [whose] wail of anguish," according to temperance literature, was "wafted over an otherwise happy land."

The main arguments made by the crusaders about the victimization of women were the following: men who drank spent money on liquor that should have been spent at home; time that men spent in the saloons was that much time away from home. Crusaders and other temperance advocates believed that alcohol was addictive and debilitating and that it impoverished families by destroying men's ability to work. Finally, they argued that drunken men were violent, likely to beat their wives and perhaps children or other members of their families as well. Alcohol, they claimed, turned gentle fathers and husbands into brutes.

While there was some truth to these allegations, it was also true that such problems were more likely to be critical in the families of the poor than among the professional and business families of so many of the crusaders. The crusaders were impelled not so much by personal histories of suffering as by a more amorphous set of fears about family life generally, fears that were too indistinct to be formulated directly but that could find some expression around the issue of alcohol. Alcohol highlighted women's vulnerable position within the family and made it possible to talk about that vulnerability without directly attacking men or challenging the structure of the family.

Crusaders dramatized their cause by telling stories about the baleful effects of men's drinking on family life, the most prominent theme being the impoverishment that men's drinking brought and its effects on dependent wives and children. The ragged and hungry wives and children of drunkards, the widows and orphans of men who had died of delirium tremens, figured in many crusader stories. Mother Stewart, a crusade leader, told the story of a case she used to gain an audience for temperance:

The fore part of this month a woman came to me, saying friends had sent her. . . . (It was the old, old story repeated—Oh, who knoweth how many times!—of wretchedness, woe, misery, privation, neglect, want, pinching poverty, and disgrace for her and her children.) . . . This woman . . . was of an old, respectable Virginia family, . . . but unfortunately married a man who soon developed an appetite for liquor. He had drifted from one place to another till her family had about lost sight of her. When she came to me she, with her three very bright children, was living in a poor tenement in one of the poorest quarters of the city. Her neighbors and only associates were of the lowest class of foreigners, and, like herself, cursed by the drink.[30]

Mother Stewart found the woman a lawyer, and, taking the woman's children with them, the three proceeded to court. The drunkard's wife was aware of her shabby appearance and was embarassed to appear dressed as she was, but, Mother Stewart wrote, "I told her not to mind, it was just as I would have it." And in her plea to the court Stewart emphasized the poverty of the woman and her children, pointing to their inadequate clothing and contrasting their appearance with that of the saloonkeeper, who "had robbed them of their protector and provider, [and] sat there so comfortably muffled up in his heavy overcoat."[31]

The issue of alcohol also made it possible to dramatize the physical vulnerability of women in the family, their inability to protect themselves from abusive husbands. Mother Stewart told a story of a woman who appeared at her door with a small child; this woman also had come from a wealthy family and had married a man who turned to drink and who had consequently taken to beating her. The woman, Mother Stewart wrote, had finally become afraid for her life and fled her home, taking her child with her, but she lived in fear that her husband might find her. "She would do anything," Stewart wrote, "would go out to domestic service if only she could find shelter for herself and child. Reason was so nearly dethroned, and the fear that the husband would come and rob her of her child . . . that if the bell rang, or she heard a step on the veranda, she would clutch the child and hasten to a place of hiding."[32]

Routinely, temperance literature blamed the alcohol, not the man, for violence committed while drunk. Temperance writers made frequent reference to the power of alcohol to turn men who were responsible and kind while sober into violent brutes, inaccessible to conscience or reason. John Gough, a temperance lecturer, told of having been approached by "a lady of aristocratic bearing" who said to him,

"You have had great experience, but have you ever known or heard of a son striking his mother?" "More than once," I said, "but never unless that son was influenced by drink; indeed, I cannot believe that any young man, in his sober senses, would strike his mother." She seemed relieved to know that hers was not a solitary case, and she informed me that she had a son who had been dissipated for years.[33]

The issue of men's drinking heightened women's sense of vulnerability within a competitive and increasingly stratified society as well as within the family. Women could not themselves engage in the competition for wealth; their social status was determined by that of their husbands. Since a woman was in most cases tied to her husband for life, marriage was something of a lottery: the young man one married might become successful enough in his work to maintain a family in some degree of comfort, or he might not, in which case his failure, if severe enough, could drive his family out of their former society, as in Mother Stewart's examples. Even if this happened only rarely, men's drinking gave crusade women a way to talk about the issue of social mobility and women's passive and vulnerable place within it, and the cause of temperance gave women some small role in keeping their men from sliding downward in the social scale.

Many temperance stories played on this theme, contrasting the comfort and respectability of the temperate man's family with the shabbiness and social isolation of the drunkard's family. Mrs. Leavitt, for instance, a leader of the Cincinnati Woman's Crusade, told of a woman who called on her one morning, carrying a six-week-old baby. The woman complained that her husband was "drinking himself to death," that the rent went unpaid, and that there was no food in the house. "He has a good trade," she said, "but all his earnings go to the saloon on the corner near us; he is becoming more and more brutal and abusive. We seem to be on the verge of ruin. How can I, feeble as I am, earn bread for myself and children?"

Mrs. Leavitt offered to call on the woman's husband and attempt to convert him to temperance, and the woman gave her consent. When Mrs. Leavitt called, she told the drunkard that on the way to his house she had passed the saloonkeeper's house and had seen his daughter, wearing white shoes, a white dress, and a blue sash. She noticed that the drunkard's daughters were shabbily dressed. She concluded, she said, that the drunkard loved the saloonkeeper's daughter better than his own, for his money was going to pay for the saloonkeeper's daughter's fine clothes. This argument persuaded the drunkard to sign a temperance pledge and to swear to keep it. Mrs. Leavitt concluded her story:

A family altar was built, the comforts of home were soon secured—for he had a good trade—and two weeks after this scene, his two little girls came into the Sunday school, with *white shoes* and *white dresses,* and *blue sashes* on, as a token that his money no longer went into the saloon-keeper's till.[34]

The temperance movement of the mid-nineteenth century produced a large number of popular novels, and the theme of the destruction of the family through alcohol was central to this literature. T. S. Arthur's *Ten Nights in a Bar-Room*, the most widely read temperance novel of the nineteenth century, told the story of Joe Morgan, a likable but weak-willed man, who frequented a saloon run by the hardhearted, money-grubbing Simon Slade. Gradually Joe became addicted to alcohol and lost whatever will he had once possessed. Devoid of ambition, he became increasingly unable to work. While his wife and daughter Mary looked on helplessly, Joe suffered through recurring bouts of delirium tremens. In the central scene of the novel, Mary, entering the saloon to beg her father to come home, was struck in the head by a beer mug, thrown at her father by Slade. Soon after, Mary died of the injury. Within a few days, Joe had died as well, a victim of delirium tremens. Joe's wife was left a widow, childless and impoverished.[35]

In the context of discussing men's drinking, it was possible for women to talk about their own isolation and loneliness. Nineteenth-century middle-class men were expected to regard their activities outside the home as the most important and meaningful parts of their lives; it was probably common for men to feel somewhat out of place in the home, which after all was understood as the woman's realm, and to prefer the company of other men. Women could hardly object to their husbands' involvement in their work, since women's livelihood depended on it, but they could object to their hus-bands' socializing with other men in their free time. The saloon thus became the symbol for the larger issue of the exclusion of women and children from men's lives. When placed in this light, the difficult issue of the structure of the economy, the distortion of human relations caused by the division between family and productive work, could be avoided, and women's isola-tion could be seen in a morally charged and personally immediate way: drinking caused men to abandon their families. One of the crusaders' songs concerned the plight of the deserted wife and children of a drunkard:

Father, dear Father, come home with me now,
The clock in the steeple strikes one,
You said you were coming right home from the shop
As soon as your day's work was done.
Our fire has gone out, the house is all dark,
And Mother's been watching since tea,
With poor brother Benny so sick in her arms,
And no one to help her but me.

Father, dear Father, come home with me now,
The clock in the steeple strikes three,
The house is so lonely, the hours are so long,
For poor weeping Mother and me!
Yes, we are alone, poor Benny is dead,
And gone with the angels of light,
And these are the very last words that he said:
"I want to kiss papa good night."[36]

Temperance literature blamed alcohol for all of the violence and neglect that took place in nineteenth-century families. This was a comforting fantasy: alcohol was more tangible and therefore easier to deal with than the larger causes of family conflict. When placed in this light, the troubles experienced by Americans in the late nineteenth century took on clear colors: it was a question of strength versus weakness, good versus evil. The good women of the temperance movement were rescuing weak men from the evil of drink. This fantasy had an appeal very similar to that held out by earlier evangelical movements, the prospect of salvation through repentance. In both scenarios, women's anger and desire for greater power were obscured by images of piety and good works. The temperance movement also gave women an opportunity to explore at least one part of the world that nineteenth-century men inhabited. The fact that temperance brought them in contact with the most forbidden part of that world may well have enhanced the attraction.

Temperance was an attractive issue for women because men's drinking symbolized so many of the injustices that women felt, and also because men's drinking posed many real problems for women in late-nineteenth-century America. The weakness of the temperance argument was that it considered alcohol in isolation, extracting drinking from its social and historical context. In fact, by the time of the Woman's Crusade, drinking had declined considerably in the United States from the first few decades of the nineteenth century. Standing at 1.9 gallons per adult fifteen years or over in 1870, consumption was at almost its lowest point since census measurement had begun in 1790. Consumption in 1870 was considerably lower than the range of 5.8 to 7.1 gallons per adult fifteen years or over per year that had prevailed from 1790 to 1830. Consumption of alcohol in 1870 was also probably considerably lower, per capita, than it had been for most of the eighteenth century.[37] Why, then, did middle-class women turn to a demand for temperance in such large numbers in the late nineteenth century?

The Sources of the Women's Temperance Movement

Temperance grew from a few voices of ministerial concern to a huge mass movement over a period during which per capita consumption of alcohol was steadily declining. This fact in no way dampened the enthusiasm of the temperance movement, which, by the late nineteenth century, held as its goal not merely less drinking but none at all. This suggests that levels of drinking that had been generally acceptable in eighteenth-century America were no longer tolerable to large groups of people in the nineteenth century. One reason for this was that drinking patterns had changed. In the seventeenth and eighteenth centuries people drank alcohol at home and at community celebrations as well as in taverns, and taverns themselves had a different atmosphere then than in the nineteenth century. Although they were frequented primarily by men, they were not male enclaves; traveling couples and families also sought meals and lodging in them. In the nineteenth century, outside of immigrant communities, drinking moved from the home to the tavern and increasingly became a men's occupation, with taverns serving as a male refuge. Furthermore, some historians and sociologists argue that drinking was more regular and lighter in the eighteenth century than in the nineteenth. In the latter period, it is argued, men might drink less regularly than had their forebears, but when they did drink they were more likely to go on binges, leading, possibly, to antisocial behavior.

This explanation, of course, begs the question: why had drinking patterns changed? The answer is rooted in the large social and economic transformation that the American Northeast experienced during the nineteenth century. The drinking patterns of eighteenth-century America were part of a preindustrial pattern of life. In the relatively sleepy economy of eighteenth-century New England, work could often be interspersed with drinking without much harm being done; artisans, farmers, even merchants could afford to work at what was often a fairly relaxed pace. In the more lively and competitive economy of the early nineteenth century, success, or even staying abreast, required more diligence and discipline, and temperance came to be a symbol of the qualities that middle-class people and some skilled workers cultivated in their quest for success and, eventually, of the qualities that capitalists sought to instill in their workers in the quest for profits. The antebellum temperance movement, which was dominated by men, first created an arena in which middle-class men could support one another in cultivating and affirming the importance of self-control; in the decades immediately before the war, when manufacturing increased significantly, it provided a vehicle for the indoctrination of the same values in working-class men. Weaning men away from centuries-old habits was a major task. Women, who never, at least in American history, had been as attached to drinking as men and who had an obvious stake in the success of their husbands, were enlisted in the task of driving alcohol out of the realm of respectability, in particular the home.[38]

Once drinking was defined as a violation of the accepted moral code, one drink could lead to a binge, and a binge could lead to other violations as well. The association of antisocial behavior gave women more reasons to oppose drinking. A man might combine drinking with a visit to a prostitute, especially since saloons were often linked to houses of prostitution; he might go home and beat his wife. By the same token that abstinence was a symbol of the iron discipline required especially of middle-class men in everyday life, drinking was associated with the temporary abandonment of this code. One infraction easily led to another. This does not mean that for all nineteenth-century men one drink led inevitably to a drunken orgy, a visit to a prostitute, or wife beating. What it means is that the danger of these things happening was greater than it had been in an earlier period.

The temperance movement published evidence that wife beating was associated with men's drinking: in 1834 Samuel Chipman, an agent for a New York temperance society, visited jails, asylums, and poorhouses throughout New York State and in some neighboring states. At each institution he obtained a signed statement from the supervisor concerning the reason for each inmate's incarceration and the state of sobriety or drunkenness of that inmate at the time of admission. Chipman's conclusion was that drunken men abuse their families, especially their wives. The following are sample reports:

ALBANY COUNTY: "Of the intemperate, at least twenty have been committed for abuse to their families."

ALLEGHENY COUNTY: "Of the intemperate, three for whipping their wives—one charged with poisoning his wife—two for arson—one for abuse to his parents."

BROOME COUNTY: "One of the intemperate was committed for whipping his wife; and two on charges of rape."

COLUMBIA COUNTY: "Fourteen were sent here for whipping their wives, or otherwise abusing their families; one of the fourteen was committed seven times for this offense."

NIAGARA COUNTY: "Of the intemperate a considerable number have been committed repeatedly; one man has lain in jail for two-thirds of the time for three years past, for abuse to his family when intoxicated; when sober, is a kind husband and father."[39]

Chipman's reports do not, of course, tell us how many sober men were incarcerated for beating their wives or children, nor do they give us any hint of how many men beat their wives or children without being incarcerated. Middle-class men, for instance, were much less likely than the poor to find themselves in jails or asylums either for drunkenness or for abuse to their families. Nevertheless, the fact that drunken men who were incarcerated had often abused their families suggests some connection between the two kinds of behavior at this time.

In both the middle class and the upper levels of the working class, temperance was a source of conflict through the nineteenth century. Working-class men took sides both for and against temperance. Middle-class men were less likely to openly fight the temperance movement than to acquiesce to the removal of alcohol from their homes and quiety go on drinking in the saloons, trying to maintain a balance between sobriety and discipline at work and the need for release after work. The reasons that the temperance movement came to be dominated by women in the late nineteenth century had more to do with the fact that middle-class women had acquired the sophistication and self-confidence to take on secular issues than with any special urgency related to the question of male drinking at that particular time. In the late nineteenth century, the question of alcohol became a source of conflict between the sexes, with immigrant men strongly opposing the temperance women, and native-born men, especially those of the middle class, taking an ambivalent stance—if in support of temperance leaving the active role in the movement to women, if in opposition expressing their views through private behavior rather than public action. Some middle-class men who supported temperance raised, at least at first, some objections to women's public activity on behalf of it. For the middle class generally, the conflict over cultural issues that, since the early part of the century, had been waged over the question of temperance now became intertwined with gender conflict. The overlaying of these issues seems to have made it difficult for many middle-class men to take any clear stand, while at the same time making it possible for middle-class women to pursue what they regarded as their interests with a great sense of moral legitimacy.

In taking over the leadership of the temperance movement, women were playing a dual role. On the one hand, they were helping to complete the cultural transformation begun largely by men in the early part of the century, creating a definition of "respectable" or acceptable middle-class behavior that was far removed from the preindustrial culture of the previous two centuries. At the same time, they were defending what they regarded as the interests of women against what they saw as the irresponsible behavior of men. Temperance women would have expressed this by saying that their mission consisted of a general defense of morality and a particular defense of women.

By the late nineteenth century, the issue of alcohol was as charged for many middle-class women as the issue of religion had been for their grandmothers. The crusades released some of the same kind of energy that had been released by religious revivals at an earlier time. One woman, signing herself "a Chastened Crusader," described her experience in the crusades in a letter to an Ohio newspaper:

The infectious enthusiasm of these meetings, the fervor of the prayers, the frankness of the relations of experience, and the magnetism that pervaded all, wrought me up to such a state of physical and mental exaltation that all other places and things seemed dull and unsatisfactory to me. I began by going twice a week, but I soon got so interested that I went every day, and then twice a day and in the evenings. I tried to stay at home to retrieve my neglected household, but when the hour for the morning prayer meeting came around I found the attraction irresistible. The Crusade was a daily dissipation from which it seemed impossible to tear myself. At the intervals at home I felt as I fancy the drinker does at the breaking down of a long spree.

The woman's husband began to look to other women for companionship, and when one of her children became sick with scarlet fever she left the crusade.[40]

At an earlier period women had to a large extent taken the defense of religion as their special task, and women's right to participate in revivals had become an issue in many families. During the Woman's Crusade, large numbers of women claimed the same mission in regard to temperance work, and at least in some families this claim to a call to activity outside the home also became an issue. Mrs. Eliza Thompson, the leader of the Hillsboro crusade, was spurred by her husband's opposition to participation in the campaign. As Mrs. Thompson told the story, she happened to be at home on the evening when Dio Lewis gave his lectures in which he urged the women to take action against the saloons, but her teenage children attended, and when they returned home they told her about the lecture, adding that the women present had hoped that Mrs. Thompson would join them in a campaign the next day. In her memoirs, Mrs. Thompson described what ensued:

My husband, who had returned from Adams County Court that evening and was feeling very tired, seemed asleep as he rested on the sofa, while my children in an undertone had given me all the above facts; but as the last sentence was uttered, he raised himself up upon his elbow and said "What tomfoolery is all that?" My dear children slipped out of the room quietly, and I betook myself to the task of consoling their father. . . . After some time my husband relaxed into a milder mood, continuing to call the whole plan . . . "tomfoolery." I ventured to remind him that men had been in the "tomfoolery" business a long time, and suggested that it might be God's will that the women should now take their part.[41]

The next morning Mrs. Thompson joined the women and proceeded to take charge of the campaign. The story of this disagreement between Mrs. Thompson and her husband became part of the folklore of the women's temperance movement. At the 1877 national convention of the Woman's Christian Temperance Union, Frances Willard recalled the incident on the occasion of presenting Mrs. Thompson with a "crusade quilt" in honor of her early contribution to the movement. Willard said,

I am reminded at this moment of how you started this mighty ball a-rolling. When you told your husband, he said to you, "It's all tomfoolery, Eliza," and you replied to him that the men had been monopolizing this tomfoolery so long it was about time the women were taking a hand.[42]

Again in a manner reminiscent of the earlier revival movement, the women of the crusades regarded themselves as representatives of the forces of good and their opponents as representatives of evil. One temperance historian gave the following account of a confrontation between a group of crusaders in Wheeling, West Virginia, and a Mr. Laramie, the manager of a "theater" in which liquor was sold, dances were held, and prostitution was arranged:

At the third of the meetings in this theater, Mr. Laramie . . . said, "Now, ladies, I have heard your side and treated you with respect. Now I want you to hear my side." He came forward with a document in his hand, which he read. It was full of the most insulting and abusive statements. He advised the women to go home and mind their business. But the women were unmoved, for they felt that their business just then was to close up that den of vice and rescue the souls he was dragging down to death.

After Mr. Laramie had finished reading the statement, one of the women went up to him, took him by the hand, and said,

"My brother, I have one request to make of you: I want you, before you sleep tonight, to take that paper and get down on your knees and ask God to forgive you for that false and insulting statement. . . . I beg you, my brother, to give up this warfare against God and humanity." The man was so deeply moved that tears streamed over his face and he promised her he would seriously consider the matter.[43]

In the communities where crusades took place, the contest between temperance and the saloons tended to become a public issue; temperance and antitemperance slates vied for office, public officials took positions, and each side held public meetings. The crusaders tended to see the struggle as one between good and evil, between refined femininity and a vulgar version of masculinity. This attitude was so pervasive that it colored the accounts of crusades given by male temperance supporters. A reporter for the *Cincinnati Commercial*, for instance, gave the following description of an anti-temperance meeting that he covered:

The meeting this evening in opposition to the women's movement, was a success as to numbers, but in nothing else. Soon after dark, the crowd began to set towards the City Hall, and in a short time a tumultuous mass filled the room with the steam of beer and the fumes of vile tobacco. I saw a dozen or twenty women walk up to the door with escourts, then pause suddenly, and after a hurried consultation, turn away with that peculiar look people have when they get into the wrong pew. . . . But the crowd, the masculine crowd! Such fearful old mugs, such low-browed, stubby-haired sons of humanity as filled the front seats, it would be hard to equal anywhere outside of the large cities. I was particularly struck with the appearance of one genius with a roaming red nose, pig eye and soap-fat chin, who held an enormous cane in his hand and started the applause. . . . Taken as a whole, I could never have believed that the fine, old respectable city of Chilicothe could have vomited forth such a crowd. If any unprejudiced visitor could have seen both and compared this with the [temperance] meeting on Thursday evening, I think he must perforce have come out convinced that the wildest vagaries of the praying women's movement were simple, cold indifference compared with what the situation called for.[44]

The issue of temperance was particularly compelling for middle-class women of the late nineteenth century because it touched on many issues that were central to their lives. The vision of a husband who unaccountably became a drunken brute, driving his family from middle-class respectability into poverty and social isolation, had a particular resonance among women who were entirely dependent upon their husbands, who in marrying had tied their own fortunes to the unpredictable futures of particular men in a highly competitive and uncertain milieu. As drinking came to be associated with wife beating, neglect, and desertion and alcohol became the symbol of a strain of masculine hostility to women and the family, temperance became the obvious terrain of women's defense of home, family, and the values associated with that realm.

The Woman's Crusade was part of a long-term process by which middle-class women gained the strength to act on behalf of what they perceived as their interests. A history of religious activity had helped to give these women the skills and confidence necessary to mount an organized defense; through the crusades, women began to explore the possibilities of taking the offensive against forces that threatened them in a way that had not been possible as long as religion had set the limits of respectable women's activity.

The outlook that shaped the crusades and formed the basis of temperance ideology had its roots in a period when the main tensions that middle-class women had experienced had been between themselves and their men. While class differences certainly existed in early-nineteenth-century America, they rarely impinged in any direct way upon these women's daily lives: their world view was circumscribed by their own communities, in which the tone was firmly set by the Protestant Anglo-Saxon middle class. In the late nineteenth century, the demands of American industrialization, mass immigration to the United States, and the growth of an American working class began to pose a different cultural threat to the women of middle-class communities.

At the same time, the crusades expanded the horizons of the middle-class women who participated in them. They began to feel their collective power, and what had been a rather amorphous, if widely shared, set of moral values began to take shape as a social outlook and a guide to women's action. But the crusades also helped to create a sharp division between these women and those of the emergent working class. In any event, there would have been large differences between these two groups; immigrant women as a whole were not likely to adopt many of the tenets of middle-class women's moral and religious outlook, nor were they likely to understand their conflicts with their own men in the same way that middle-class women did. The fact that temperance was made a cutting edge of the outlook of middle-class women reflected a preoccupation with class differences and sharpened the antagonisms between middle-class and working-class women.

CHAPTER FIVE

The Woman's Christian Temperance Union and the Transition to Feminism

THE WOMAN'S CRUSADE subsided after less than a year. Such intense activity could not be maintained, especially on the basis of purely local organization. But the issue itself was not by any means exhausted. The Woman's Crusade had only begun to tap the concern of middle-class women over the question of alcohol. The crusaders had made no systematic effort to broaden their movement, and they had spoken only in passing of the larger social issues to which temperance was linked. The crusades had found support among many women who were not actively involved in them, and their demise stimulated widespread thought and discussion about the future of women's temperance activity.

The Woman's Christian Temperance Union followed the crusades, and through diligent organizing and by appropriating to itself the charisma of the crusades, the WCTU was able to grow to a membership of over 176,000 by the turn of the century; through the last two decades of the nineteenth century, it was the largest American women's organization of that time or earlier. The WCTU replaced the loose network of Woman's Crusade groups with a tightly knit but democratic national organization and it broadened the scope of the movement by making the connection of temperance to larger issues more explicit, especially such issue as the defense of the home and the advancement of women.

Within the WCTU, the values and attitudes that had informed female evangelism and the Woman's Crusade were carried forward, sharpened, and made the basis for social and political action. Like their predecessors, the women of the WCTU saw social morality as inextricably tied to Protestant religiosity, and they believed that it was the duty of women to uphold moral and religious standards. The sensibility of the women of the WCTU, like that of their predecessors, was shaped by an antagonism to men, or at least to the masculine culture that seemed to threaten female piety and religiosity. The

Woman's Crusade was the first step toward a secularization of what had been a church-centered women's culture, and in the last two decades of the century the women of the WCTU continued the process. While the women's culture that guided the WCTU remained highly religious, its focus of activity shifted out of the church into social reform.

It was within the women's temperance movement of the late nineteenth century, in particular the WCTU, that the tradition of female religious enthusiasm was transformed into an explicitly political set of concerns, centered around but by no means limited to the issue of alcohol and its effect upon women and the home. Frances Willard, the president of the WCTU from 1879 until her death in 1898, played a central role in this politicization of women's culture. She successfully fought for a linkage between temperance and woman suffrage, arguing that only the vote could give women the power necessary to eradicate alcohol. She also fought, with some success, to develop the protofeminist elements of the women's culture that the WCTU had inherited. While avoiding the language of feminism, she initiated discussion within the WCTU about female equality in the home and outside it. She outlined what she regarded as a feminine vision of social order, a vision that was critical of industrial capitalism and had much in common with utopian socialism. This vision found support among the women of the WCTU, in large part because it was limited to the values of social harmony, altruism, and service to society that framed women's culture.

While the stands taken by the WCTU represented only the membership of the organization—and often not the entire membership—in a more general sense the WCTU can be taken as barometer and to some extent molder of the opinions and outlook of the native-born Protestant women of the Northeast and Midwest, especially what might loosely be called the middle-class women of this group. These were the women whose roots lay in the Protestant churches, whose history led back to the evangelical movements of the early part of the century. The composition of the WCTU in the last decades of the nineteenth century reflected the geographical and occupational trajectory of the groups that several generations earlier had entered commerce and trade in the northeastern towns, especially in New England. In the late nineteenth century, the WCTU was strongest in the midwestern "New England belt" and in the northeastern states themselves, and it was centered in the large towns and growing cities rather than in the countryside.[1] The WCTU also included other groups, of the same Protestant background but of somewhat different class location: in areas of the Midwest the membership of the WCTU overlapped significantly with that of the People's party.

By the turn of the century, the WCTU had developed a quite broad appeal, especially among native-born Protestant women. But the founders of the organization were from the social group that liked to describe itself as "respectable," meaning that the men of their families made a fairly comfortable living, usually as part of the commercial or professional stratum or as skilled workers, and that their families were Protestant and traditionally churchgoing. The leadership of the WCTU continued, over the last two decades of the century, to speak most easily to and in the name of such women.

The Early WCTU: The Victory of Woman Suffrage

From the inception of the WCTU, the issues of social reform and women's advancement were intertwined with the question of temperance. In 1874, as the last crusades were subsiding, a National Sunday School Assembly was held in Fairpoint, New York, that drew churchwomen from the Midwest as well as from New York State and New England. Many of the women who attended that meeting had themselves been involved in the crusades, and they enthusiastically endorsed a proposal for a women's temperance organization that could draw women out of the home while at the same time furthering the fight against alcohol.[2] Later that year, 135 women from sixteen states, most of them from the Midwest and Northeast, met in a Presbyterian church in Cleveland to found the National Woman's Christian Temperance Union.

The women of the NWCTU agreed that their main goal was the fight against what they called "the rum curse," but agreement as to methods was not so easily reached. Should the WCTU restrict itself to education and persuasion, or should it demand legal prohibition and try to enter the political arena so as to influence legislation? Should it confine itself to the issue of alcohol, or should it extend its concerns to the reforms that many of its members regarded as linked to temperance? Annie Wittenmyer, the first president of the union, held the conservative position, believing that the organization should restrict itself to the question of alcohol and to the traditional female methods of persuasion and prayer and should eschew demands for legal prohibition or involvement in politics in any way. Her position corresponded with an organizational conservatism: Wittenmyer and the women who surrounded her favored the exercise of strong central authority, in effect a veto power over local or state unions that might wish to pursue broader goals through unorthodox methods. Because she feared the expansive mood of the membership, Wittenmyer did little to foster the growth of the WCTU. Discomfort with her heavy-handed leadership, frustration over her failure to exploit the movement's potential, and growing disagreement with her social conservatism all created the basis for a challenge within the WCTU.[3]

The first challenge to Wittenmyer's policies came from Frances Willard, a prominent member of the Illinois union. When Willard entered the WCTU, the progress of women was her main concern. She was attracted to the WCTU as much by the prospects it held for organizing women to advance their own cause as by her commitment to temperance.[4] Willard's challenge to Wittenmyer came over a demand for a limited form of woman suffrage. "Local option" laws enabling local elections on questions of the licensing of saloons and the enforcement of prohibition had for decades been a target of temperance activity, and Willard suggested that the WCTU should press for the opening of these elections to women. In the summer of 1875, she influenced the Illinois union to pass a resolution stating that, "Since woman is the greatest sufferer from the rum curse, she ought to have the power to close the dramshop over against her home."[5] Later that summer, she heard a speech on the same subject by a Canadian temperance woman who used the term "Home Protection ballot," and Willard adopted this phrase as her slogan.

Willard's fight for the "Home Protection ballot" won support within the midwestern state unions but met strong opposition from the national leadership and at first failed to find support among the eastern unions. At the convention of 1875, Willard was publicly denounced by the president of the New York State union for introducing a resolution for the Home Protection ballot and was privately reprimanded so sharply by Wittenmyer herself as to be forced to resign her office of national corresponding secretary. Soon thereafter, Willard was elected president of the Illinois union and from that position she continued to press for her program. In 1877 the Illinois union circulated a Home Protection petition to the state legislature, for which it ultimately obtained the signatures of 180,000 men and women. The petition was tabled by the Illinois state legislature but made its real impact within the WCTU. Embarrassed by its popularity within the organization she led, Wittenmyer circulated a Home Protection petition of her own that resembled Willard's in requesting the cooperation of the state in the fight against alcohol but differed in that it failed to mention woman suffrage in any form.[6]

Willard and her supporters continued to campaign for their program at the national conventions of the WCTU. In 1875 and 1877 resolutions were put forward endorsing the Home Protection ballot, and in both cases, after debate, the resolutions were approved. Though the Wittenmyer faction had editorial control of the WCTU's house organ, then called *Our Union* (later the *Union Signal*), Willard had been made chair of the publishing committee in 1876, when the paper was on the verge of financial disaster. After reorganizing it successfully, she proceeded to use it as a vehicle for prosuffrage articles, over the protests of the editors. This issue was brought to the national convention in 1878, where the paper's editors, with Wittenmyer's support, argued that references to woman suffrage should not be allowed in the pages of *Our Union* because the WCTU was not in favor of suffrage and there was no popular interest in the subject. Willard argued that while women of the East were not interested in suffrage, women of the West were strongly in favor of it:

A Baltimore lady said to me yesterday: "Persimmons are nice when they are ripe, but they pucker the mouth when they are green." This Home Protection Petition is a green persimmon in Maryland, but, my friends, it is a ripe one yonder on the prairies, and you surely wouldn't forbid us to gather and partake of it?[7]

Though it was true that the prosuffrage faction in the WCTU was stronger in the Midwest than the East, Willard's emphasis was shaped as much by political exigencies as the desire for accuracy: the eastern state unions were not likely to condemn a program associated with a section of the country that was vital to the growth of the WCTU. In fact, prosuffrage opinion was growing in the eastern unions in response to Willard's campaign. At the national convention of 1879 the suffrage faction won a decisive victory within the organization: Willard was elected president, a post she held until her death.

Frances Willard's victory signaled a period of rapid growth for the WCTU. As of 1879, the membership of the organization numbered only

27,000 in a little over a thousand locals in twenty-four states. By 1883 there were over 73,000 members, the number of locals had more than doubled, and the organization was represented in forty-two states. By the turn of the century, membership had reached more than 168,000 in over 7,000 locals, and the WCTU had at least some presence in every state. Willard's encouragement of expansion and her desire to incorporate all reform interests within the WCTU were probably significant factors in the growth of the organization. It also seems clear that the feminist politics engaged in by the WCTU under her leadership contributed to its growth; women were attracted to the opportunity to engage in reform activity, and especially reform activity shaped by a concern for the interests of women. The WCTU's appeal was due not just to its moral conservatism but to its support of reform and woman suffrage in the context of that stance.

It is difficult to estimate what WCTU membership meant for most women in the years when Willard was president. The only requirements for membership were regular payment of dues and adherence to the temperance pledge. Though officially all members were attached to locals of the WCTU, there is no way of knowing how many women attended meetings or how often. Willard and the WCTU leadership generally understood the impor- tance of meetings in fostering loyalty to the organization and conventions were therefore dramatic and festive occasions that attracted thousands of women. Union publications give the impression that membership was taken relatively seriously; stories are told about pressure being brought to bear on women who failed to attend meetings or shirked their share of the work. This impression is reinforced by the high turnover rate of the national membership—as much as a quarter of the members in a given year—sug- gesting that inactive members did not remain with the organization and that the WCTU was not isolated but supported by a very large number of sym- pathetic women.[8]

Female Reform, Political Action, and Suffrage

Willard's election demonstrated both widespread discomfort with Witten- myer's narrow conception of the women's temperance movement and enthusiasm for the Home Protection ballot. Willard moved to consolidate this enthusiasm and extend it to woman suffrage and a general openness to reform by announcing what she called the "Do-everything policy." This policy relaxed central control within the WCTU and endorsed virtually anything that state or local branches of the organization might choose to do in pursuit of temperance or related issues. As the "do-everything policy" was put forward at the national convention of 1881, it included but did not require participation in campaigns for woman suffrage:

Resolved, that wisdom dictates the Do-everything policy: constitutional amendment, where the way is open for it; Home Protection where Home Protection is the strongest rallying cry; Equal franchise, where the votes of women joined to those of men can alone give stability to temperance legislation.[9]

The do-everything policy signaled the decisive shift from Wittenmyer's conception of a movement devoted strictly to temperance to a vision of a general women's reform movement, focused around but not limited to the issue of temperance.

Endorsement of woman suffrage was the most controversial aspect of this policy within the WCTU. Seventeen women left the organization over this issue,[10] while many reported virtual conversion experiences in which they reached the conclusion that it was their duty as Christian women to demand the vote, abhorrent as they found such an idea.[11] Many probably remained agnostic, but the great majority were either convinced of the necessity of suffrage in some form or at least willing to remain in an organization that included suffrage in its program. Over the years, interest in suffrage grew. Many state unions participated in campaigns for state and municipal suffrage, often contributing substantially to the work of women's suffrage organizations. As the weakness of local option laws made it evident that strategy was insufficient for the WCTU's ends and as the prospects for woman suffrage were enhanced, enthusiasm grew. In 1892 Anna Shaw, an early WCTU member and now a leader of the suffrage movement, addressed the WCTU's national convention and was received with enthusiastic applause and the waving of white handkerchiefs. Taking over the platform, Willard said, "Shoo, ladies; this is different from what it was in Washington in 1881 when you refused to let me have Miss Anthony on my platform. Things are coming round, girls."[12]

The do-everything policy facilitated not only the growth of support for woman suffrage but a gradual shift within the WCTU to active involvement in politics. Large numbers of WCTU members, like northerners generally, gave their support to the Republican party; sectional political allegiances were part of the legacy of the Civil War and colored American politics through the latter part of the nineteenth century. In addition, the Republican party generally was more favorable to temperance than was the Democratic party. In 1880 the WCTU gave its support to the Republican candidate, James A. Garfield, and when he failed to carry out his temperance pledges, disappointment was widespread. WCTU members' readiness to draw away from support of the Republican party was reinforced by their perception, widely shared among reform forces of the time, of the Republican party's opportunistic "waving of the bloody shirt," its willingness to use popular northern sentiment arising out of the Civil War for its own political purposes.

While many women within the WCTU remained staunchly Republican, the growing disaffection of others led them to look toward the formation of a third party as a force for reform within which the WCTU could exercise real influence. Thus, when the National Prohibition party, which included the demand for woman suffrage in its program, appealed to the WCTU for support, the opportunity was taken up readily. Willard and others organized a Home Protection party—outside the WCTU but made up in large part of its members—arguing that this step would permit the women to enter the Prohibition party on the basis of organized strength and give them leverage for their demands. In 1882, when the two organizations fused, the women insisted that the new organization be called the Prohibition Home Protection party, both in an effort to gain the support of the WCTU as a whole and to make sure that women's stake in temperance would be featured prominently in the program of the new party.[13] It seems likely that Willard and her immediate supporters used this sequence of events mainly as a strategy for winning the WCTU over to the third-party movement. At a time when women did not have the vote, a political party made up of women made sense more as a way of bringing women into politics than as a way of exerting women's influence on the political process.

The WCTU's influence in the Prohibition Home Protection party was not lasting; in 1884 the men of the new party were able to change its name back to the Prohibition party. The party's support of woman suffrage was too weak for the taste of some WCTU members,[14] and in any event the party itself never became strong enough to realize its goals. In 1892 Willard tried again. She entered the Populist movement and chaired the first convention of the People's party, hoping to bring about a fusion with the Prohibition party and to induce the new organization to support both of her prime demands. But the Prohibitionists were reluctant to fuse with the Populists, the Populists were unwilling to endorse either prohibition or woman suffrage, and the voteless women of the WCTU had no significant impact on the outcome of the convention.[15]

Whatever the impact of the WCTU on the third parties of the time, involvement with these and other reform organizations had an important effect within the WCTU itself. Both the Prohibitionists and the Populists associated themselves with wide-ranging programs of social reform, and as the WCTU increasingly looked to these and other such groups for alliances, the discussion of temperance and woman suffrage in the WCTU was increasingly likely to be placed within a broader social context. Not all members of the WCTU supported this development. In 1889, when the national convention officially gave its endorsement to the Prohibition party (though carefully avoiding any implication that WCTU members were required to give such support), a second small group of women left in protest, this time numbering thirteen, slightly less than the group that had left over the union's support of woman suffrage eight years earlier. These were Republican women; their protest was directed more against the WCTU's association with the third-party movement than against woman suffrage. Most WCTU members were at least willing to go along with the increasing involvement of their organization in progressive politics. By the end of the 1880s, radical ideas were obtaining a widespread hearing within the WCTU: the populist language of opposition to privilege could be found regularly in the WCTU press, and Frances Willard and others were arguing in favor of public control of industry and other such reforms through the *Union Signal* and at national conventions.

Contact with other reform groups helped the WCTU to broaden its outlook over the 1880s, but the fundamental impulse toward transforming the organization from a women's temperance to a women's reform organization came from within the WCTU itself. During the seventies the Wittenmyer leadership had tried to confine the activities of the WCTU to temperance alone and as a result had lost control of the organization. The do-everything policy that Willard put forward in 1881 encouraged expansion of the WCTU's concerns. Under Willard, the WCTU required only that members abide by the pledge of abstinence and pay their dues. The latitude granted state and local unions to construct their own programs allowed reform programs going beyond temperance to flourish, and Willard herself encouraged such expansion by establishing national departments in areas of WCTU concern. Through the 1880s and 1890s countless departments were established, which Willard attempted to classify under the general headings of temperance, women, labor, and welfare, but these designations were more reflective of the WCTU's expanding concerns than of the orientation of particular departments, many of which spanned two or three of these categories. Every time a new department was established, some effort was made to defend it in terms of its relevance to temperance, but since Willard and the leadership of the WCTU generally saw the question of alcohol as intertwined with every conceivable social problem, there was virtually no area of reform work that could not be defended on this basis. The proliferation of departments reflected the breadth of the WCTU and the diversity of outlooks represented within it. While some departments continued along entirely conventional lines, others pursued goals that remained subjects of debate.

The least controversial of the WCTU's departments were those concerned directly with temperance activity, such as the Department for Temperance Work among Negroes and Foreigners and those concerned with activities that were regarded as entirely respectable, such as the Flower Mission, which delivered flowers to invalids and inmates of institutions. The Department of Scientific Temperance Instruction provided educational material about the dangers of alcohol and pressed, often successfully, for the election of temperance advocates to school boards and for the inclusion of temperance material in schoolbooks. The Department of Health and Hygiene conducted campaigns to educate women on the need for exercise, proper diet, and comfortable clothing. The Kitchen-Garden Department conducted classes in cooking for young women, not only to train them to cook for their families but also to enable them to find domestic work. The Kindergarten Department sponsored a string of kindergartens, where the children of working mothers were cared for and, of course, exposed early to temperance propaganda.

The more controversial departments were those whose work took them directly into politics or led them to advocate views that were not fully accepted within the WCTU. The Suffrage Department conducted state and municipal campaigns for the woman's vote, often in coordination with the women's suffrage movement. The Politics Department encouraged and organized WCTU participation in campaigns of the National Prohibition party. The Department of the Relation of Temperance to Labor engaged in conventional temperance activities in working to persuade trade unions to require temperance of their members and employers to discriminate in favor of abstinent workers, but less conventionally, it also conducted a campaign within the WCTU to create an understanding of industrial conditions and sympathy for the cause of labor, especially of working women and children.

Victorian Morality and Prowoman Politics

Everything the WCTU did was informed by a moral stance shaped by commitment to what were perceived as the interests of women and by an antagonism to what was seen as a masculine culture. This element of sexual antagonism was most apparent in the work of the Department of Social Purity, also called the Department for the Suppression of the Social Evil, which was among the most active of the WCTU's departments. Formed in 1883 in response to newspaper stories describing the enticement of girls and young women, this department attacked the "social evil" of prostitution that for the most part the women of the WCTU could not bring themselves to name. The main obstacle to such work was the widespread taboo among "respectable" women against discussing such a subject; Willard and others argued vehemently that such delicacy was a luxury that the WCTU could not afford.[17] Through this department, the WCTU conducted a nationwide campaign for state laws raising the age under which girls could be legally protected from such seduction. This was one of the organization's most effective campaigns; by 1894, it could boast of having raised the "age of protection" throughout the United States to an average of fourteen years.[18]

Many of the goals of the WCTU overlapped with those of other reform movements of the period. Prohibition, woman suffrage, even the suppression of prostitution, were goals subscribed to by a wide range of organizations in the late nineteenth century. What differentiated the WCTU was the attitude it brought to these reforms: in every aspect of its work, it kept uppermost its concern for women, framed in terms of its own understanding of women's interests. In the case of prostitution, the WCTU directed its energy toward working for laws that would make it possible to prosecute men who lured women into prostitution or profited from it, while maintaining an attitude of sympathy for the women themselves, as long as they condemned prostitution and regarded themselves as victims of an evil system. Frances Willard, who headed the Department of Social Purity for a time, recommended that every local union appoint a woman to assist women accused of prostitution in what she called the

terribly unequal banter of the courts . . . for in those courts a man's testimony is not invalidated because he is a libertine, but if a woman is unchaste she is practically disqualified as a witness, except in a case where her testimony favors the man's side, whereupon a jury of men will naturally accept at par value.[19]

Letters to the *Union Signal* agreed that the blame for prostitution should be laid in the right quarters. One letter condemned the "double standard . . . [according to which] the man may do with impunity what renders woman an outcast from society," and the widespread complicity of women who would receive "the impure man as an honored guest in her parlor, while she would refuse to allow his victim to earn a living scrubbing her kitchen floor."[20] Another letter argued that by shunning prostitutes rather than the men who frequent them respectable women allowed themselves to be divided from their sisters:

Consider the great underlying fact in this whole dreadful business, the fact that womanhood is divided into two distinct and hostile bands. One, inside the walled fortress of home, is protected, is respected, is beloved and honored. The other, having passed the gateway by a single sin, . . . is thrust without the wall. . . . And between these women and those within home's fortress, pass and repass, welcome both ways, men, the most respectable in reputation and position, the most blessed in powers and opportunities, the most blessed in legitimate domestic relations.[21]

In the same spirit, the women of the Iowa WCTU put these sentiments into practice by securing a law requiring that "men who frequent the haunts kept by degraded women shall be punished as felons."[22]

The WCTU's efforts to require of men the conduct expected of women went beyond the issue of prostitution and into the relations between the sexes in everyday life. Willard coined the phrase, "the white life for two," which she called the supreme goal of the WCTU and the crowning achievement of reform. Though she was never indelicate enough to spell out exactly what "the white life" entailed, Willard seems to have meant not only virginity before marriage but minimal sex within marriage as well. She advised women to say to their suitors, "You must be as pure and true as you require me to be, ere I give you my hand," and she wrote,

There is no man whom women honor so deeply and sincerely as the man of chaste life; the man who breasts the buffetings of temptation's swelling waves, like some strong swimmer in his agony, and makes the port of perfect self-control. Thank God, in spite of all the accursed latitude, how many men are pure and true![23]

Under the aegis of the Department of Social Purity, the WCTU inaugurated an organization for men, the Society of the White Cross, and for boys, and Knights of the Silver Crown. Men were required to take a pledge, promising "to treat all women with respect . . . to maintain the law of purity as equally binding upon men and women . . . to use all possible means to fulfill the command, 'Keep thyself pure.'"[24] The pledge for boys required avoidance of "impure" thoughts or discussion. Organizers of boys' groups were instructed to avoid being too explicit about what this meant and under no circumstances to conduct such discussions when girls were present.[25] There is no record of the number of men and boys who joined these societies, but the frequent references to "the white life" in the *Union Signal* indicate that the goal was popular among the women of the WCTU.

Frances Willard's failure to spell out the meaning of "the white life" was not simply a matter of delicacy. The WCTU's quest for "the white life," for "social purity," was a symbolic crusade for the transformation of American life that could no more be reduced to the specifics of sexual relations in marriage than could the quest for temperance be reduced to the cessation of drinking. The white life meant establishing an equality between the sexes by bringing both men and women under the sway of Victorian morality; it meant elevating the position of women by placing restraints upon sexuality, supposedly a primarily male interest, and valorizing the moral role of women in family and society. The argument that the sexes should be governed by the morality espoused by middle-class women merged with the argument that men should become more like women, more nurturing and sympathetic. Men, it was felt, should take a larger role in family life and parenting, while in politics and the marketplace competition and greed should be replaced by harmony and altruism so that women might enter and participate with comfort and dignity.

Frances Willard, and undoubtedly other WCTU members as well, saw the white life as linked to the struggle for dignity and equality for women. Outside the home, women's freedom of movement would be enhanced by a single standard of morality that would protect women from men's advances; within marriage, the white life for two would enable women to limit the number of children they bore. Willard saw the subjugation of women as linked to an oversexualization of relations between the sexes; she related this to alcohol by arguing that drunken husbands were likely to force themselves upon their wives, leading, she believed, to the birth of deformed children. Willard spoke of "the awful crime of enforced motherhood which is every day casting insane, idiotic and criminal children upon society to wreak their vengeance upon the heedless source of their misery and degradation. . . . So long as it is possible for one child to come into the world by accident, or against the will of either parent, the sexual pandemonium which disgraces our boasted civilization will be perpetuated."[26]

The connection she drew between a woman's unwilling participation in sexual intercourse and the birth of "idiotic and criminal children" had of course no basis in fact. Social purity and the goal of the white life bespoke the deep fear of sex inculcated in middle-class women from an early age. At the same time, the ideas of social purity reflected more than the extremity of Victorian hostility to sexuality; they also reflected an understanding that sex was a crucial area in the conflict between men and women, that women were made subordinate to and dependent upon men in sexual activity and through pregnancy and childbirth. The WCTU's attitude toward sex contained elements of political acumen as well as fear.

Home Protection and Protofeminism

The WCTU defended Victorian morality and fought for its extension in the belief that it was in the interest of women. The slogan of Home Protection was the link between the Victorian morality and the "prowoman" stance of the WCTU. Home Protection meant an attempt to enforce a moral code that was frequently repressive. The WCTU conducted campaigns against plays and books it found offensive, applauded the work of Anthony Comstock and his Society for the Suppression of Vice, and, in the late 1890s, took up a campaign for curfews for young people. (Partly as a result of wctu efforts, curfews for people under eighteen, and in some places up to the age of twenty-one, were imposed in 4,000 towns throughout the United States.[27] The wctu believed that any steps in the direction of greater sexual freedom would undermine family life and would work to the detriment of women, but in its efforts to protect family life, it undertook to police morality, women's as well as men's.

The wctu saw the defense of the family, and its own espousal of a moral code that it believed would contribute to such an effort, as of central importance to women generally. The organization believed that poverty was the main threat to the home but that what it regarded as male irresponsibility was a crucial contributing factor. Men's power over dependent women and children could easily be abused, while men's ignorance of or insensitivity to the needs of families meant that family issues could be neglected in a society run by men. The women of the wctu believed that only female equality would ensure responsible male behavior and give family issues their proper place in public life. Articles in the *Union Signal* pointed out that women had little recourse when mistreated by drunken husbands and argued for woman suffrage on grounds that the vote would enable women to protect family life. As usual, Frances Willard made the argument most pithily, pointing out that a male electorate could be induced to support laws for the protection of virtually every industrial interest—land grants for the railroads, tariffs for manufacturers, subsidies for steamship companies—but that only a female electorate would see to it that laws were passed for the protection of the family.[28]

A cogent argument often put forward in defense of woman suffrage was that the course of modern civilization made it imperative; where at one time families had enjoyed a sphere of autonomy, the intrusion of the state into all areas of life weakened families and women's position within them. Women's organized power and in particular female suffrage were necessary to rectify the balance. Frances Willard argued,

The home was once almost a world apart in which the outside state interfered but little. In that home woman was queen. Now that kingdom has been invaded, her crown despoiled, her very children taken possession of by the state. These changes were inevitable. With the progress of civilization the claims of society grew. . . . But woman, the dethroned queen, demands and has a right to demand that her position of equal authority in the home be recognized in the state.[29]

On a less abstract level, the argument was put forward that increasingly women shared with men the costs of the state and therefore ought to share in determining its course. "Women have felt the pressure of civil government very heavily in this country, over the last twenty years," one letter to the *Union Signal* argued. "They gave fathers and brothers, husbands and sons, to die in a political war . . . [they have been] driven to self-support, their burdens have been increased by excessive taxation. . . . The conviction is rapidly gaining ground that women ought to be more than the victims of government."[30]

The women of the WCTU believed that their organization furthered the cause of women not only by pressing what they saw as women's issues but also by helping to create organized bonds among women, thereby increasing their power. In 1891 the *Union Signal* asked a number of leading members of the organization to respond to the question, "What has the white ribbon done for you?" Edith R. Archibald answered, "More than any other force in the world today, has the magic of the white ribbon seemed to develop the *comradeship* of women and their loyalty to each other." Frances J. Barnes wrote, "When I see the white ribbon on one in female garb, no matter what her style, or how poor her apparel, I at once say, 'there is one of my sisters, a woman who belongs!'" Esther Pugh answered,

The space alotted would be insufficient to tell what the white-ribbon movement has been to me personally. In the death of mother and father, in surrendering a home, in the breaking of the family circle, in the uprooting of social life and setting aside the ties of blood, in the mutations which always come with the years, it has stood with me for Penates, for hearth, for friends, for all that goes to fill the life and heart of a woman. . . . The personal relationships which have come into my life through it are stronger than death.[31]

Stories in the *Union Signal* identified the white ribbon with women's power and often stressed its ramifications for struggles between husbands and wives. One story concerned a WCTU member whose drinking husband ridiculed her temperance activities. One day a thief entered their home, tied up the husband, and was preparing to tie up the wife when he noticed the white ribbon pinned to the woman's hat. Stopping short, he announced that his mother, when she was alive, had been a member of the WCTU and had taught him to always respect a woman who wore the white ribbon. Seizing the opportunity, the wife instructed the thief to untie her husband. Soon the three were seated around the dinner table, the husband joining the would-be thief in praises of the WCTU and promising to help the man find a job so that he would no longer be forced to steal.

In another story a man named Tom Burton consistently left his wife Jennie and their small baby in the evenings to join his friends, often at the local saloon. One evening, driven to despair by loneliness, Jennie followed her husband to the saloon. Tom, ashamed, led Jennie home, where she suffered a breakdown. For weeks all she could say was, "I'm—so—lonely, I'm so lonely." Eventually she regained strength and was able to leave her bed; the first evening that she was able to come to the dinner table, she found Tom and his drinking companions seated around it. Tom addressed his friends: "Boys, when a man does a wrong action publicly, it's his duty to confess publicly. . . . I will say nothing of the wrong done my dear ones, but, thank God" (here tears appeared in Tom's eyes) "with His help, I will throw off the power that could have destroyed my soul and body. I want to commit myself—I want it to be no secret—from this day, I mean to be a decent man." Tom held up a copy of the WCTU's temperance pledge and said, "I want to sign this in your presence." Tom's friends followed him in signing the pledge, and the story ended as follows:

Right doing seems not to impair digestion, for that dinner party was a success! Often after this these five men met at Tom Burton's and brought their wives. Sam Thirsty [the saloonkeeper] wondered not a little that they never came and after numerous attempts to lure them back, gave them up for lost. Mrs. Burton archly alludes to the experience of that night as "her spree," but her husband gravely says, "it was, for me, well-nigh a Waterloo."[32]

To some extent, women of earlier generations had found female comradeship in the church and female power in the appeal to religious morality, but the sense of strength in female collectivity was greatly enhanced in an organization of and for women, one in which women could gain confidence through public activities and internal leadership and support in far-reaching bonds with other women. These ties were the basis of both benevolence and enhanced power. The WCTU often described itself as "organized mother love," and Frances Willard happily quoted her sister-in-law as saying that the WCTU was like "having a score of mothers for every boy."[33] As the organization gained public influence, men began to ask why they were not allowed to join. In 1892 Willard defended the exclusion of men from the organization:

"Why do not women open their great and successful philanthropic and other societies to men?" is a question we begin to hear asked by the best and most liberal-minded among our brethren. The answer is that these organized movements are, as we think, God's great recruiting stations for the new war in which He is enrolling, drilling and disciplining. If men were at the front of these societies, as they would necessarily be if there at all, women would not develop so rapidly, or become so self-respecting and individual in character: they need to learn how to use the weapons with which the future is certain to equip them. . . . We work alone in order to become experts so that we can hold our own when we go into societies with men. . . . They would not have received us on terms of equality if we had come to them before we could bring trained minds and well-seasoned experience. We must first show power, for power is always respected.[34]

The WCTU was correct in seeing itself as upholding the interests of women, but only in the very narrow sense that it accurately reflected what was at least very widespread, possibly majority, opinion among late-nineteenth-century American women. If American women had had the vote at this time, there is every reason to believe that they would have voted as the WCTU said they would, casting their ballots in larger numbers than men for temperance, for welfare legislation that would enhance family life, and in support of the moral code the WCTU favored, particularly if white Protestant women had voted in larger numbers than black or immigrant or Catholic women, as would likely have been the case. The immediate effects of the female vote might well have been approved by the WCTU, but on a deeper level there was a contradiction within the union's argument. The WCTU supported both conventional morality and women's equality, and ultimately the two were inimical. Conventional morality and, for that matter, Home Protection implied the defense of what was in fact a male-dominated family structure. Though it was immediately in the interest of women to defend the family, since it was their only refuge in a male-dominated society, and though it was understandable that many women would fear anything that seemed to threaten that structure or their accustomed place in it, ultimately female equality implied criticism and restructuring of the family. The WCTU was "prowoman" or "protofeminist" in that its politics were framed by women's concerns about their place as women in family and society. It fell short of genuine feminism in that for the most part it merely reflected women's immediate, and often contradictory, sense of what would be best for them given a male-dominated family and social structure. Victorian morality, for instance, might serve the interests of at least some women in a society in which women suffered an extreme sexual vulnerability to men; but sexual repression hardly constitutes female liberation. In crucial ways the WCTU assumed rather than criticized male dominance and as a result was unable to put forward more than a few elements of a feminist vision.

The contradictions inherent in the attempt to simultaneously support conventional morality and female equality emerged in the WCTU press in the course of a discussion about the proper content of marriage vows, which expanded into a heated debate over the question of divorce and the WCTU's attitude toward it. On January 24, 1895, the *Union Signal* printed a letter describing a feminist wedding ceremony that had been held in the home of the author, Rachel Foster Avery. The letter was entitled "Olive Shreiner's Dream Realized":

On the last day of 1894, at the home of Mr. C. Miller Avery and Rachel Foster Avery, at Somerton, Pa., a thoroughly equal rights marriage ceremony was performed. The couple were a Mr. Raymond W. Smith . . . and Miss Eleanor E. Shaw, and the Rev. Anna Howard Shaw performed the ceremony for her niece. But the young people certainly took matters, at least in part, in their own hands. . . , They married each other by their own spoken words. . . . The phrasing of their mutual vow was of their own arranging, and was perhaps more radical than the participants themselves realized; it was exactly the same for both. "I, Eleanor, take thee, Raymond, to be my husband. I promise to be to thee a loving and faithful wife so long as thou art worthy of the trust which I this day place in thee, and with this ring I seal my vow."

Such marriages as these, and the assumption of such entirely mutual obligations, presage the better time for both men and women, when the tyranny of sex shall have become a thing of the past.[35]

This "equal rights ceremony" brought a heated response. A letter from a woman by the name of Anna Carpenter criticized the ceremony as not only un-Christian but antiwoman. Scorning the designation of such a ceremony as "equal rights," she wrote, "There are those who fail to recognize in this enlargement of liberty the . . . advantage secured to the wife. May not the man . . . find in the terms of this partnership, a ready door out of obligation by declaring his wife unworthy of the trust placed in her? Surely," she concluded, "woman should hold inviolate the inspired Word. No other rock has ever yielded leverage for her uplift from misery and thralldom.[36]

Rachel Foster Avery responded in the next issue, arguing to the contrary that the majority of divorce proceedings were initiated by wives, on grounds of cruelty, desertion, and drunkenness. What the WCTU should oppose, Avery argued, was not divorce but divorce law, which as it stood allowed much wider latitude to men than to women.[37] Against Avery's argument, another WCTU member pressed a feminist argument for narrow grounds for divorce:

I do not suppose that Mrs. Avery, or those who agree with her, follow their teachings to their logical conclusions, but I cannot think of anything more dangerous to home and to society. . . . Whatever breaks down the home, hurts woman most, because she is most dependent upon home affections for her happiness. . . . There are no true friends of the real advancement of woman who would attempt to loosen the bond of marriage or to make it anything less than the lifelong union of one man and one woman.[38]

Finally, the editorial board of the *Union Signal* took a stand, attempting to defend marriage and stay within what they regarded as Christian law, which allowed divorce only in the case of adultery, but at the same time to support the rights of wives against their drunken husbands. The *Union Signal* found the resolution to this quandary in the renunciation of sex and in what amounted to an antidivorce position:

We do not say that there are no cases where a separation is desirable upon other grounds than that of infidelity,—though we think the circumstances are rare which justify such breaking up of a home—but a separation of this kind is not "divorce" and does not necessarily "loosen the marriage bond." Indeed, a legal separation which forbids the marrying again of either party during the lifetime of the other, tends rather to emphasize its indissolubility.[39]

Though the editors of the *Union Signal* were unwilling to endorse the liberalization of divorce law that Rachel Foster Avery indicated and reluctant to deviate from the accepted Christian belief that only adultery should constitute grounds for divorce, they were nevertheless disturbed by the law's inequity. The members of the WCTU recognized that women were often forced into bad marriages by economic necessity and might find themselves tied to drunken brutes for the rest of their lives. In 1886 the *Union Signal* editorialized that, as long as saloons were left open, drunkenness should be grounds for divorce.[40]

A decade later the *Union Signal* placed the inequities of the divorce law within the context of the historical subordination of women:

It is now admitted that the first form of divorce was what is known as the matriarchal, that is, the power of divorce lay entirely in the hands of the woman, the father had no rights to his children. A change came about which completely reversed this condition of things and placed all family power in the hands of the man. . . . This was caused by the custom which obtained of men capturing in war maidens whom they held as wives but at their own option could divorce. From that time, men have held, in most unfair degree, the control of divorce customs. The committee on divorce [of the WCTU] represents no stated views as to the grounds upon which divorce should be granted. Its sole purpose is to grant for women an equal power concerning divorce laws.[41]

In spite of its recognition that the difficulty of obtaining a divorce might trap women in unhappy marriages and that existing divorce law treated women unfairly, the WCTU was unwilling to support any liberalization, which it considered incompatible with its understanding of Christian morality and the defense of the home. The suggestion that Home Protection and the defense of women's interests might not always exactly coincide emerged also in WCTU discussions of marriage. In May of 1889, the *Union Signal* conducted a symposium on the question, "Is marriage a failure?" Respondents unanimously insisted that their own marriages were not failures by any means, and all of the men who answered described the institution of marriage itself as entirely successful. The women were not so sure. Mrs. L. M. N. Stevens, for instance, after describing her own marriage as blissful, mentioned a young couple of her acquaintance. The husband drank, while the wife was temperate. For the husband, she wrote, the marriage was a success. "He certainly does do much better than he used to do before he was married. For her it may be doubtful.[42]

The WCTU was willing to recognize that marriage did not ensure happiness for women and that a single woman could be as useful to society as a wife and mother. In 1888 the *Union Signal* wrote in defense of women who remained single:

Nothing could have a more degrading effect upon the character of woman than the belief that her only way to a comfortable subsistence is marriage; that she is born not to any independent dignity and usefulness in life, but only to complete and embellish the existence of some as yet unknown man. And when we consider what a lottery is marriage, how uncertain that it will be happy . . . it becomes apparent that nothing can be more paralyzing to the nobler energies and instincts of womanhood, than that she should be limited to this one precarious chance for happiness and usefulness.[43]

In light of such discussion, it is striking that the WCTU never qualified its identification with the goal of Home Protection. Because most American women of this time, especially those who made up the constituency of the WCTU, regarded their interests as synonymous with the interests of the "home," it was possible for the WCTU to see itself as defending women and family simultaneously. When, as in the discussion of divorce, contradictions appeared, the WCTU did not hesitate to place family integrity above a woman's desire to leave her family. Similarly, the WCTU did not hesitate to call for the imposition of a moral code that it regarded as supportive of family life, even though it inhibited the behavior of large numbers of women, not only prostitutes but working-class and other women who took a somewhat more relaxed view of sexuality than did the WCTU.

When questions concerned with public life or work outside the home were considered, the WCTU did not face the contradictions it occasionally encountered in the areas of family life and morality; here the organization was able to pursue what its members called "the advancement of women" unambiguously and with great enthusiasm. The WCTU publicly called for the opening of every "respectable occupation" to women as well as men, and at the same pay;[44] it protested the exclusion of women from juries and hinted broadly at the nefarious motives that might drive men to such exclusion.[45] The WCTU engaged in campaigns for the hiring of female police officers, so that women who were arrested could deal with women rather than men;[46] it pressed for the opening of official positions within the churches to women and waged an active and partially successful campaign for the ordination of women ministers.[47]

Frances Willard expressed most forcefully the commitment of the WCTU to the equality of the sexes. In her address to the national convention of 1895 she denounced the belief that women might be in any respect less than men's equals, calling such ideas ignorant and incompatible with democratic values. She argued that the only fundamental difference between the sexes lay in women's ability to be mothers and men's to be fathers. She called for a society in which men and women would be regarded as equal in all respects and suggested that such a change would mark a new stage of civilization:

In primitive days we had the matriarchate which means the rule of the mothers, and now for a painfully lengthened period we have had the patriarchate or the rule of the fathers, but we begin to see the dawn of the amphirate or the joint rule of a joint world by the joint forces of its mothers and its fathers. Happy are they who put their willing sturdy shoulders to the wheel of this white chariot of the Sun.[48]

The WCTU and Labor

For the leadership of the WCTU and many of its members, Home Protection led not only to an insistence upon equality for women but also to an identification with labor and an openness to or support for socialism. Through the 1880s and into the 1890s the WCTU maintained a close relationship with the Knights of Labor, the largest and most important labor organization in the United States until it was overshadowed by the American Federation of Labor.[49] The bond between the WCTU and the Knights was based on a similarity of outlook, especially on the part of the leadership of the two organizations.

The Knights of Labor had highly diverse aims, membership, and organizational forms; by the 1880s it included skilled artisans, semiskilled workers who were in many cases threatening the position of artisans with industrialization, some unskilled workers, and some middle-class people who saw the Knights as a vehicle for reform. The organization included both trade unions and mixed assemblies, where membership was based on geographic location irrespective of occupation. The Knights of Labor functioned as a trade union, as a cooperative or benefit society, as a secret society based on religious ritual, and as a force for moral and political reform around such issues as land control, currency, taxes, and temperance. It was also an educational society: members studied such topics as political economy, cooperation, and current political issues. Virtually every social theory then circulating among the labor, reform, and third-party movements was held at some time by some group within the Knights of Labor: cooperation, greenbackism, the single tax, utopian socialism, temperance.

The Knights of Labor encompassed contradictory beliefs about trade unionism and contradictory social philosophies. Knights differed about whether strikes were or were not proper or desirable trade union actions, and though large numbers of Knights espoused socialism, the term was applied to contradictory social visions. Some of these ideas can be seen as shaped by the immediate past. The Knights of Labor derived from a number of secret labor societies that had managed to survive the depression and failed strikes of the seventies largely because their secrecy made them difficult to destroy. When these societies came together as a national organization in 1879, they brought with them a dual legacy—a radical critique of capitalism and a fear of strikes. The horrors of the early years of industrialization had encouraged a hope that industrialism might be a passing nightmare, that capitalists and workers could be replaced by masters and apprentices and class conflict by class harmony. Their experience in the seventies had led the societies that made up the Knights to see strikes as at best a financial drain and at worst a threat to the existence of the labor movement. In the eighties these attitudes persisted, especially among the leadership of the Knights of Labor. Opposition to strikes was also endorsed by the nontrade elements within the Knights, who did not wish to contribute to strike funds. At the same time, changing conditions were encouraging new ideas among the rank and file, especially those who belonged to trade assemblies. With the greater prosperity of the eighties, the strike appeared to many Knights as a useful weapon. Evidence was mounting that neither the process of industrialization nor the class polarization and conflict that accompanied it could be reversed. These trends encouraged a more modern socialist outlook, a hope that the working class would gain the power to end the wage system and establish a classless society.

Terence Powderly, who headed the Knights in the 1880s, strongly adhered to the older of these sets of ideas: he proclaimed his disapproval of strikes, explaining that a society based on the harmony of classes could be better attained by a policy of class cooperation than by class conflict. In spite of such proclamations, Powderly and other leaders of the Knights were in fact equivocal; pressure from within the Knights, and the logic of capital-labor relations in the eighties, propelled them toward endorsing the strikes that their social philosophy disapproved. The Southwestern Railroad strike of 1886 took place under Powderly's leadership and with his reluctant approval. The failure of the Knights in the late eighties can be traced on the most immediate level to the failure of that strike and to the Haymarket labor demonstration of the same year, in which a bomb was thrown, probably by a provocateur, at ranks of police, thereby identifying the labor movement with violence and turning substantial segments of public opinion against it. On a deeper level, the organization's demise may be traced to its division on crucial issues; the necessity for labor conflict was eroding the older ideology of cooperation, and the adherence of the leadership to that older ideology prevented it from giving the organization the direction it needed.

The goals that Powderly espoused, including a society in which class conflict would be replaced by class harmony and a sober and respectable working class with the moral self-discipline to achieve that society, were quite attractive to the women of the WCTU. Beyond this, the Knights and the WCTU were able to work together because they shared a commitment to a series of reforms, though sometimes for different reasons. The Knights supported prohibition, woman suffrage, and the equality of women in the labor movement. Powderly was not willing to require abstinence as a condition for membership in the Knights, but he lent support to the WCTU's argument that temperance was in the interest of working people. In 1886 Powderly gave his personal support to the WCTU campaign to raise the "age of protection," not only signing the petition but sending it with his endorsement to every local assembly. The WCTU's goal of "Sabbath reform," to encourage the observance of the Sabbath through the passage of laws requiring that shops and places of amusement be closed on that day, was also endorsed by the Knights, though as much out of the desire to gain a day's leisure for working people as out of moral concern.[50]

Many WCTU members, in addition to sharing Powderly's desire for a society in which class harmony would replace class conflict, shared with the Knights generally a desire to see the end to the exploitation of labor by capital. This orientation coincided with the WCTU's interest in moral and social reform, but interest in the conditions of working people and sympathy with the goals of organized labor was encouraged by the WCTU's association with the Knights. In 1888 the *Union Signal* published a series that stressed the oppression of women and children in the factories, and other pieces also protested the injustices of a class society. In an article entitled "justice for the Sewing Woman," A. B. E. Jackson wrote:

What is my relation to the woman who makes the garments I purchase? would perhaps be a profitable question for all women to ponder. It would certainly lead many to a knowledge of facts . . . startling and pathetic. . . . If in addition to the feeling of indignation and pity, came one of determination to leave no stone unturned until these poor, ill-paid and ill-fed creatures received a fair remuneration for their labor, great good would be the result. It certainly requires no vigorous thinking to discover the fact that the makers of garments, sold at the low figures at which they can now be purchased, receive the merest pittance for long hours of labor.[51]

While some WCTU members gave support to the cause of labor against that of capital, a larger number deplored the social conditions that set the two against one another and believed that temperance would serve the interests of both and reduce the occasions for conflict. This attitude was not so prevalent in discussions of the large capitalists, who were engaged in sharp conflict with labor and for whom WCTU members would have been slower to express sympathy, as it was in the case of the small businessmen who, along with working people, suffered severely from the depressions of this period. During the depression of the mid-nineties, the *Union Signal* ran articles describing alcohol as bad for both business and labor. The sale of alcohol, one such article argued, drew resources from legitimate enterprises and impoverished honest businessmen, while the consumption of alcohol depleted workers' already insufficient resources. If only the money spent on alcohol were directed elsewhere, as would be the case if the saloons were closed, "immediately there would be such a revival of business interests as has never before been seen." Prohibition, the article continued, would help capitalists by providing them with more productive workers, and it would also give workers strength in their struggles with the bosses. "The use of alcoholic liquors robs labor of the clear brain that is necessary to contend with capital. . . . Not only is the liquor traffic the enemy of the laboring man, but it is the enemy of the capitalist as well."[52]

The assumption that the depression of 1894 was a bad thing for both labor and business, especially small business, and that both shared an interest in the return of better times was certainly correct. What is open to question is whether an end to the sale and consumption of alcohol would have had the revitalizing effect that the author envisioned. The article reflects the uncertain attitude of many WCTU members toward the labor conflicts of the time. On the one hand, there was within the WCTU considerable sympathy for labor in its struggles with capital, especially big capital, which was often seen as gouging the public generally as well as exploiting labor. On the other hand, many WCTU members were also sympathetic to the interests of capital, especially if that meant small businessmen, and for moral reasons if not out of class solidarity shared with them the desire for sober and industrious workers.

Nevertheless, the WCTU found in its support for family integrity a powerful reason to support the demands of the labor movement. The most important of these demands, in the late nineteenth century, were a "living wage," which would enable male workers to support themselves and their families in some semblance of comfort, and the eight-hour day. Both demands expressed the needs of working-class families as much as those of individual male workers, and the WCTU supported them out of recognition that adequate income and leisure were necessary for secure family life. At the national convention of 1892, Frances Willard spoke on the relation of Home Protection to labor. Anything that worked to destroy the home, she said, the WCTU must oppose; because family life required fathers as well as mothers, working hours that kept men absent from the home for long periods must be fought. "This it is which compels us to take up the labor question; this it is which compels us to identify the cause of women with the cause of labor everywhere."[53]

Through the 1890s Willard continued to argue that the central problem facing the family was that of father absence. "'One swallow does not make a summer,' and one parent by the hearthstone does not make a home. We need to stop singing the old ditty 'What is the home without Mother,' unless we add, 'The Father alone can make the house home.'"[54] This was an argument for closing the saloons so as to force men back into the home; it was also an argument for supporting the eight-hour day. Sabbath reform was a step in the right direction, Willard argued, but it was not enough.

We believe in parentage; we are for . . . widening the conception of the responsibilities of fatherhood. . . . God is the father, but how many families there are where the prototype of the divine is practically absent from Sunday to Sunday. We must get fatherhood, both divine and human, back into the life of the world, not only on Sundays but on every day of the week. This makes the WCTU support as a matter of principle, as a root question, all attempts to shorten the worker's day."[55]

The WCTU's support of labor, in a period when labor was in sharp, often violent, conflict with capital, represents a breakthrough of enormous importance. First, it showed an impressive ability on the part of WCTU women to transcend their own class position. While the WCTU was not an exclusively or narrowly middle-class organization, the middle stratum constituted its main social base. A narrower vision than that held by the WCTU in these decades might well have led these women to translate their concern for respectability into a support for the status quo and into a view of labor organizations as troublemakers. Second, the reasoning behind WCTU support for labor—the understanding that shorter hours and better pay would enhance the family lives of working people—suggests an understanding that poverty, in combination with the capitalist organization of work and the economy, was the fundamental cause of the weakness of family life. Such an understanding places the question of irresponsible male behavior in a different context from that often assumed by the WCTU, for Willard's argument that long hours and low pay undermined the working-class family suggests that the fundamental problem was the structure of society. By supporting the demands of an overwhelmingly male labor movement, Willard and the WCTU implied that men's actions in their own interests could at the same time be actions on behalf of family integrity.

The WCTU's breadth of vision, and the belief of many of its members that a thoroughgoing defense of the family required a critical look at society, made it possible for leftist ideology to find an audience within the organization. In the late 1880s and especially in the 1890s, Frances Willard became increasingly interested in socialism.[56] In 1888 she read Edward Bellamy's *Looking Backward* and was attracted to his vision of a society in which class exploitation and class conflict would no longer exist, a society in which harmony and rational discussion would prevail over competition and the use of force. Through Bellamy, Willard became interested in the Nationalist Clubs that espoused his philosophy, and in 1889 she joined the editorial board of a Christian Socialist magazine, *The Dawn*. In the summer of 1893 Willard went to England, where she became intimate with Lady Somerset, the unconventional head of the British WCTU, and through her was introduced to and joined the Fabian Society. Socialism now moved to the center of Willard's interests. She came to see it as not only the extension but the prerequisite of temperance, the advancement of women, and the amelioration of the conditions of working people. Willard wrote that if only she were ten years younger she would devote her life to the cause.[57]

Frances Willard became interested in socialism through the Christian Socialist movement; she routinely referred to her vision of a future society as "gospel socialism" and spoke of it as "Christianity in practice." Her emphasis on the moral aspects of socialism, and her identification of it with

Christianity, undoubtedly made it more palatable to many women within the WCTU. But her understanding of the organization of a socialist society was strikingly modern; she defined socialism as "the principle of collective ownership and control of all the means of production and distribution."[58] Willard argued that the struggles for temperance and for socialism were linked, for through the liquor trade capitalists and politicians joined to keep working people down. She quoted a working woman to the effect that "poverty causes intemperance and intemperance causes poverty" and argued that only socialism could break the circle.[59] She linked her vision of socialism with what she called "the eternal feminine" and urged the women of the WCTU to lead the struggle for a society in which the values of Christianity and home life would be realized, one in which competition and exploitation would no longer exist and alcohol would find no market.

In fact, socialism provided the soundest, if not the most popular, defense of WCTU values in a period in which these values were being challenged and undermined by the advance of industrial capitalism. In large part, no doubt, because of the common ground shared by Christian socialism and nineteenth-century women's culture, a substantial number of WCTU members became interested in socialism; of these many eventually entered the Socialist party. The great majority undoubtedly remained unconvinced, but they at least listened politely to Willard's attacks on capitalism.

To speak in favor of socialism in the 1880s and 1890s was to risk association with anarchy and violence. In the middle decades of the nineteenth century, utopian or Christian socialism had been the predominant trend within the socialist movement in the United States, and this tradition had been for the most part safely confined to the intelligentsia. In the last decades of the century, variants began to emerge, especially anarchism and to some extent Marxism, and as socialism came to be associated with the often violent class conflicts of the period, it lost its reassuringly decorous quality. Because of these associations the editors of the *Union Signal* found it necessary to defend Willard as espousing a respectable variety of socialism. In response to worried inquiries from WCTU members, the *Union Signal* explained that a socialist was not the same thing as an anarchist but was "a reputable person who believes in law and order, in peace and arbitration . . . in education and the ballot box as the proper channels through which to express the people's discontent. . . . When one of our leaders recently avowed herself a socialist, she meant what we have stated."[61] When Willard and Lady Somerset went to Haverhill, Massachusetts, to publicly support a strike of women shoe stitchers, the *Union Signal* again defended them, but on the narrowest and most apologetic of grounds. The conditions under which the women worked were deplorable, the *Signal* wrote, the strike was being conducted in an entirely orderly way, and all but two of the town's seventeen ministers supported it. "It hardly need be said that we do not advocate strikes, nor do our leaders. They believe that the slower methods of agitation, education and the ballot-box must be the weapons of the working class, but this case is certainly exceptional."[62]

The *Union Signal's* difficulties in defending Willard's support for labor struggles and its insistence that her socialism had nothing to do with overt class conflict suggest that Willard's ability to take the organization as a whole with her as she moved to the left was limited. They also reflect the discomfort of large sections of the WCTU with the idea of any direct tie to the labor movement, except as mediated through an organization like the Knights, which was by the late eighties as much a reform as a labor organization, and a man like Powderly, who was seen as exerting a beneficial moral influence on workingmen. The organization's uneasiness was reinforced by its hostility to immigrants and their culture, especially Germans, although the *Union Signal* and the leadership generally succeeded in avoiding derogatory remarks about immigrants. Hoping to attract such women or at least to influence their thinking, they pointed out that not all immigrants or even all Germans drank, and they argued that those who did should be seen as victims of alcohol rather than as enemies of the temperance movement. In the same way that the WCTU could sympathize with prostitutes if they showed a desire to leave their profession, it could sympathize with people who saw their intemperance as something to be overcome. This was hardly the basis for a working relationship with the immigrant communities that constituted a large part of the late-nineteenth-century American working class.

Willard's socialist politics were never the target of any overt attack within the WCTU, but her unorthodoxy raised questions, and the decline in enthusiasm for third-party politics in the wake of the defeat of populism in 1896 helped to undermine her political influence. In the late nineties rumors circulated that Willard and Lady Somerset had been seen sharing a bottle of wine.[63] And a speech by Willard at a world temperance congress in London, in which she argued that poverty was as much the cause of intemperance as was intemperance the cause of poverty, generated protest in the WCTU press.[64] At the national convention of 1896, for the first time since 1889, substantial opposition to support for the Prohibition party was registered. Willard was by this time spending more and more time in England with Lady Somerset, and the fact that she was reelected to the presidency of the WCTU year after year testifies to her solid position in the organization as a result of two decades of work. At the convention of 1897 an attempt to unseat her failed, but she was elected by 387 votes out of 436 rather than with the usual unanimity. A year later she died.

After Willard's death the WCTU contined to drift away from active involvement in politics. The national convention of 1899 withdrew the WCTU's endorsement of the Prohibition party and did not give support to any other party. In the early part of the twentieth century all other aspects of the WCTU's work were continued, but in some areas the emphasis changed. Members in the Department of Social Purity became discouraged in their attempts to work with prostitutes, and increasingly focused their efforts within a subdivision of the department called Purity in Literature and Art. Under this slogan the WCTU conducted campaigns for censorship in public libraries, for regulation of the content of plays and films, and against women's adoption of newer, more revealing styles of dress.[65]

The growth of progressivism in the first two decades of the century did not lead the WCTU back into politics. Though ultimately the Progressive movement was a major force in the winning of prohibition, a substantial section of the movement did not favor prohibition. Many urban reformers in particular saw no harm in the workingman's habit of occasionally drinking a glass of beer and did not wish to lose what immigrant working-class support they enjoyed through association with the WCTU's brand of moral conservatism. The WCTU was seen by many people, especially in urban areas, as engaged in a fruitless attack on twentieth-century culture. While in many places the WCTU continued to grow in the first two decades of the century, joined in its quest for prohibition by the powerful Anti-Saloon League, in the context of national politics the WCTU was placed on the defensive.[66]

Earlier in its history, the WCTU had been able to create what came close to being a radical and feminist politics on the basis of the middle-class women's culture of the time. The women of the WCTU, in their attempt to translate their values into social action and to advance what they saw as the

cause of women, attained an impressive breadth of social vision, an understanding of the women's cause that in important ways transcended narrow
class identification and at times transcended even the antagonism to men
that generated their concerns. The WCTU can be seen as having pushed the
women's culture of the time to its limits. The politics of the WCTU
demonstrate not only the possibilities but the limits of a culture that
accepted the structure of the nineteenth-century middle-class family and, by
extension, the subordination of women; the WCTU went as far as it could in
pursuing the feminist and progressive possibilities of this culture. But its
primary goal was the nuclear family's monopoly of the organization of personal life, and the WCTU believed, probably correctly, that this required the
support and propagation of a Victorian moral code. It was the WCTU's
insistence on this conservative morality that limited the support it could give
to women and held it back from wholehearted support for progressive social
change.

Conclusion

THIS HISTORY of women's antagonism toward men and toward a masculine culture, as expressed through popular movements of the nineteenth century, intersects with the history of feminism. Female evangelism preceded feminism and was only indirectly related to it, but the women's temperance movement was closely connected to the women's suffrage movement of its time. The WCTU undoubtedly brought feminist ideas, especially woman suffrage, to a much broader audience than the suffrage movement itself did. Frances Willard and other WCTU women consistently supported equal rights for women in every area of public life. In addition, Willard, at least, argued that women should be trained and educated and that occupations outside the home should become available to them, so that they would not have to depend upon marriage for a livelihood. She also believed that men should become more involved in family life in general and parenting in particular and that husband and wife should treat one another as equals.

In spite of all this, Willard and the WCTU stopped short of identification with feminism. They avoided such phrases as "the rights of women," finding such language too strident, and the WCTU was never publicly allied with the woman suffrage movement to the extent that it was, for instance, with the Knights of Labor. The WCTU set itself at a distance from feminism in part because feminism was controversial; public association with the women's suffrage movement, for instance, was potentially more damaging than association with the Knights. More fundamentally, the WCTU distanced itself from feminism because it did not share the same priorities. Willard and other WCTU women supported a series of feminist demands, but more as a means of creating a higher morality than as ends in themselves. Willard herself regarded a rectification of the balance of power between men and women as valuable for its own sake, but she defended it on what she considered higher grounds, as a vehicle to the triumph of a morality based on values she associated with family life, not on a vision of equality between the sexes.

The "white life" was the embodiment of the WCTU's moral code, and the vision it described must have been attractive to many women. Under its sway, women's moral authority would be enhanced, and sexuality would be sharply delimited and made subservient to childbearing and motherhood. If men could be brought to adhere to the moral code it prescribed, women would be protected from abuse or desertion and also from venereal diseases contracted from prostitutes by their husbands. The white life was hardly likely to be realized on any large scale in the late nineteenth century. By this time Victorian morality had lost whatever chance it might once have enjoyed of being adopted by large numbers of men; in the early decades of the twentieth century, large numbers of women would abandon it as well.

The goal of social purity did not distinguish the WCTU from the feminist organizations of the time; women of the National American Woman Suffrage Association often argued for suffrage on grounds of women's superior morality, and they would have been quite comfortable with Willard's description of the white life. Ironically, it was this moral stance that served to limit the influence of the WCTU, not its flirtation with controversial movements such as feminism.

To some degree in the early twentieth century and to an even greater extent after the winning of prohibition, the WCTU suffered from its identification with old-fashioned morality. After the victory of woman suffrage, the feminist movement faced the same problem. The moral code espoused by both movements was increasingly seen as involving a self-abnegation and in particular a denial of sexuality that found less and less favor with the young women of the twentieth century. The defense of "social purity" was close to if not the central goal of the WCTU, and the organization could not withstand the transformation of the terms of discussion of morality that took place in the twentieth century. The feminist movement did not regard social purity as its first priority, but its understanding of its purpose had been shaped by an acceptance of Victorian morality, and it was unable to restate the discussion of women's interests outside that framework. As nineteenth-century women's culture became outdated, feminism became a victim of its ties to that culture.

The history of the popular women's culture and politics of the nineteenth century raises questions about power relations between men and women, about the construction of domesticity and its ideologies. This study argues that the spheres of men and women were not so separate as they seemed in the nineteenth century, that domesticity allowed for an expansion of women's moral influence, but that influence is not the same thing as power and that women's power, such as it had been in the eighteenth century, was undermined by nineteenth-century domesticity. Victorian morality was constructed within the confines of this situation and represented a defense of women's interests only within the framework of an acceptance of male dominance. For the vast majority of nineteenth-century American women, such acceptance was of course a given: only those few who were willing to forgo the benefits of marriage, or who had the luck or privilege to construct extraordinary family arrangements, were able to raise fundamental questions about the sexual hierarchy.

What is the purpose of raising questions about past movements and people that they did not ask themselves, of placing their words and actions in a framework they did not construct? First, it can help us to understand their experience more fully, and especially to understand some of the tensions in that experience. Nineteenth-century women acted within a tension between the claims of domesticity and the pulls of a society unfolding beyond the borders of the family. The definition of women's roles and of the relationship between men and women that was put forward in the marriage guides of the time, and that was probably widely accepted by middle-class people, provided an only partially adequate framework for understanding women's experience. For this reason many women were open to considering new ways of looking at family relations and the roles of women. This created the space in which it was possible for some women to sharpen the critical edge of values that women had long accepted as their own, to argue on the basis of those values for female social and political action. The strength of women's culture was that it allowed a recognition of the fact that women had a particular set of interests. The identification of those interests with a universal morality and with the institution of the family was a mixed blessing; it gave women a clear set of goals and enabled them to act with conviction, but it made it more difficult for them to criticize a family structure and a moral code that forced women into restricted roles, though it did give them a kind of security. Women's culture tended to see morality and power as separate and incompatible and to abjure the discussion of power for the discussion of morality. But women's actions were shaped by considerations of power, even though mediated through the language of morality. Adding this term to the discussion of the history of nineteenth-century American women enriches our understanding of it.

Placing past historical experience within the framework of more modern questions can also help us to distinguish between the parts of that experience we wish to maintain or revive and the parts we wish to leave behind. Nineteenth-century women's culture and feminism were shaped within the cultural milieu of the urban middle class, which perceived working-class cultures, especially immigrant cultures, in a fundamentally antagonistic way. In the early twentieth century, most of what limited organization took place among working-class women was local in scope; the initiative for such organization often came from reform-minded middle-class women, but the working-class members of such groups generally did not come into contact with the feminist movement itself in any regular way. The Women's Trade Union League was the one organization of the time that tried to confront issues of both sex and class and that brought middle-class and working-class women together in an ongoing way. The working-class women of the WTUL complained routinely about the arrogance of their middle- and upper-class colleagues, their seemingly unshakable belief in the superiority of their culture, and their tendency to identify it with the interests of women. Even those working-class women who rose to leadership within the WTUL were often unable to resolve the conflict they felt between their working-class and feminist allegiances.

The contemporary women's movement faces similar problems; because of the tremendous growth of the working class in twentieth-century America, it is now much more important that feminism find a way of encompassing class divisions. Working-class women are far more involved in the women's movement now than a century ago, especially in the National Organization for Women, but feminist program and ideology are still shaped primarily by the needs of the more privileged. Right-wing movements have been able to reach a much larger working-class constituency than feminism by focusing on demands for "the defense of the family" through an end to abortion and opposition to the ERA and gay rights.

The disintegration of family life as we know it has not been adequately addressed by feminism. The main contribution of feminism in the sixties and early seventies was the critique of family life, and so far the women's movement has not been able to integrate that critique with a positive program for a reconstruction of personal life. The question of personal life was at the center of the WCTU's concern, and some elements of a program lie in the approach it took to that question. Women's position in the family will depend, finally, upon women's organized power and upon the existence of a social order that guarantees full employment to women (as well as to men), that upholds women's equal rights in all spheres, that understands child care as a social responsibility and backs up women's demands for shared responsibility for child rearing. This vision has much in common with Willard's socialist utopia: it differs in supporting not one form of family but a wide range of forms of private life.

Notes

INTRODUCTION

1. Studies of nineteenth-century suffrage include Eleanor Flexner, *Century of Struggle: The Woman's Rights Movement in the United States,* (Cambridge: Harvard University Press, 1958); Aileen Kraditor, *The Ideas of the Woman Suffrage Movement, 1890–1920* (New York: Columbia University Press, 1965); Ellen Du Bois, *Feminism and Suffrage: The Emergence of an Independent Woman's Movement in America* (Ithaca: Cornell University Press, 1978). Du Bois's argument that the demand for suffrage was radical and feminist is stated succinctly in her article "Radicalism and the Woman Suffrage Movement: Notes toward the Reconstruction of Nineteenth-Century Feminism," *Feminist Studies* 3, nos. 1–2 (1975): 63–71.

There is a substantial literature on the daily lives of nineteenth-century middle-class American women, examining domestic work, family relations, and relations among women. Nancy F. Cott, in *The Bonds of Womanhood: "Woman's Sphere" in New England, 1780–1835* (New Haven: Yale University Press, 1977), discusses these and other areas of such women's lives; family life is evoked in Ann Douglas Wood, "The Fashionable Diseases: Women's Complaints and Their Treatment in Nineteenth-Century America," *Journal of Interdisciplinary History* 4, no. 1 (Summer 1973): 25–52, and in Carroll Smith-Rosenberg, "The Hysterical Woman: Sex Roles and Role Conflict in Nineteenth Century America," *Social Research* 39, no. 1 (Spring 1972): 652–78. Relations among women are suggested in William Taylor and Christopher Lasch, "Two 'Kindred Spirits': Sorority and Family in New England, 1839–1846," *New England Quarterly* 36 (1963): 25–41, and studied in greater depth by Carroll Smith-Rosenberg in "The Female World of Love and Ritual: Relations among Women in Nineteenth-Century America," *Signs* 1, no. 1 (Autumn 1975): 1–29. Carl Degler's "What Ought To Be and What Was: Women's Sexuality in the Nineteenth Century," *American Historical Review* 79 (December 1974): 1467–90, raises questions about the extent of the impact of Victorian morality on women, at least educated women living in the last decades of the century.

Another closely related literature examines women's activity outside the home and the moral and social values that women were exposed to, which women themselves played a major role in constructing. Kathryn Kish Sklar, in *Catharine Beecher: A Study in American Domesticity* (New Haven: Yale University Press, 1973), studies the development and internal contradictions of domestic ideology. Women's activity in moral reform is examined in Carroll Smith-Rosenberg, "Beauty and the Beast and the Militant Woman: A Case Study in Sex Roles and Social Stress in Jacksonian America," *American Quarterly* 23, no. 4 (October 1971): 562–84, and in Mary P. Ryan, "The Power of Women's Networks: A Case Study of Female Moral Reform in Antebellum America," *Feminist Studies* 5, no. 1 (Spring 1979): 66–85. Women's role in the Second Great Awakening is discussed in Nancy F. Cott, "Young Women in the Second Great Awakening in New England," *Feminist Studies* 3 (Fall 1975): 14–29, and in Mary P. Ryan, "A Woman's Awakening: Evangelical Religion and the Families of Utica, New York, 1800–1840," *American Quarterly* 30, no. 5 (Winter 1978): 601–23.

Finally, another literature, again closely related, examines nineteenth-century female sexuality and reproduction and the women's struggles that arose out of these issues. Barbara Ehrenreich and Deirdre English, in *For Her Own Good: 150 Years of Experts' Advice to Women* (New York: Anchor Press, 1978), trace conflicts between male experts and women over issues of health and family life through and beyond the nineteenth century, and Linda Gordon, in *Woman's Body, Woman's Right: A Social History of Birth Control in America* (New York: Viking Press, 1976), traces struggles over birth control for a similar period.

2. Ann Douglas, *The Feminization of American Culture* (New York: Alfred A. Knopf, 1977).

CHAPTER ONE

1. The best account of the New England Great Awakening is contained in Edwin Scott Gaustad, *The Great Awakening in New England* (New York: Harper and Brothers, 1957). Ola Elizabeth Winslow, *Meetinghouse Hill, 1630–1783* (New York: Macmillan Co., 1952), provides a framework for understanding the Awakening. The best general account is Joseph Tracy, *The Great Awakening: A History of the Revival of Religion in the Time of Edwards and Whitefield* (Boston, 1841).

2. For an account of the upheavals that took place in eighteenth-century New England, see Richard L. Bushman, *From Puritan to Yankee: Character and the Social Order in Connecticut, 1690–1765* (Cambridge: Harvard University Press, 1967), especially pt. 4, on the relationship of the Great Awakening to these tensions. For a view of the emergence of such tensions on a smaller scale, see Kenneth A. Lockridge, *A New England Town: The First Hundred Years, Dedham, Massachusetts, 1636–1736* (New York: W. W. Norton and Co., 1970), and Philip J. Greven, *Four Generations: Population, Land, and Family in Colonial Andover, Massachusetts* (Ithaca: Cornell University Press, 1970).

3. For a defense of the Great Awakening, see Jonathan Edwards, *The Distinguishing Marks of a Work of the Spirit of God, Applied to that uncommon Operation that has lately Appeared on the Minds of many of the people in New-England* (Boston, 1741). For a critique, see the writings of Charles Chauncy, especially *Enthusiasm described and caution'd against* (Boston, 1742), and *Seasonable Thoughts on the State of Religion in New England* (Boston, 1743).

4. Esther Williams's conversion account contained in "Relations of various persons who joined the church at Chebacco, 1764," Papers of Rev. John Cleaveland,

Essex Institute Historical Library, Salem, Mass. (hereafter cited as Chebacco accounts).

5. Daniel Low, Chebacco accounts.

6. Moses Holbrook's conversion account contained in Papers of the Baptist Religious Society, Sturbridge, Mass. Old Sturbridge Village Library (hereafter cited as Sturbridge accounts).

7. Thomas Prince, ed., *The Christian History* (Boston, 1743), 1:261.

8. Nathan Cole, "Born 1711 and Born Again 1741," no page numbers, Connecticut Historical Society, Hartford.

9. Hannah Bear, Chebacco accounts.

10. Elizabeth Perkins, ibid.

11. Jonathan Edwards, "Some Thoughts concerning the Present Revival of Religion in New England," in *The Great Awakening*, ed. C. C. Goen (New Haven: Yale University Press, 1972), p. 295.

12. Esther Williams, Chebacco accounts.

13. Sarah Kinsman, ibid.

14. Sarah Butler, ibid.

15. Prince, *Christian History*, 2:90.

16. Cole, "Born and Born Again."

17. Sarah Kinsman, Chebacco accounts.

18. Prince, *Christian History*, 1:262.

19. Isaac Proctor, Chebacco accounts.

20. Michael Low, ibid.

21. Lucy Proctor, ibid.

22. Merriam Marcy, Sturbridge accounts.

23. Wife of Moses Holbrook, ibid.

24. Hannah Cook Heaton, "Experiences of Spiritual Exercises," no page numbers, Connecticut Historical Society, Hartford.

25. Mortality rates in colonial America are detailed in Daniel Scott Smith, "The Demographic History of New England," *Journal of Economic History* 32 (1972): 165–83; Maris A. Vinovskis, "American Historical Demography: A Review Essay," *Historical Methods Newsletter* 4 (1971): 141–48; and idem, "Mortality Rates and Trends in Massachusetts before 1860," *Journal of Economic History* 32 (1972): 184–213. For a discussion of the relationship between actual mortality rates and New Englanders' preoccupation with death, see idem, "Angels' Heads and Weeping Willows: Death in Early America," in *The American Family in Social-Historical Perspective*, ed. Michael Gordon, 2d ed. (New York: St. Martin's Press, 1978), pp. 546–63.

26. Jemima Harding, Sturbridge accounts.

27. Elizabeth Marshall, ibid.

28. Jacob Choate, Chebacco accounts.

29. Jeremiah Kinsman, ibid.

30. Mary Shumway, Sturbridge accounts.

156 NOTES

31. John Winthrop, "A Modell of Christian Charity," Winthrop Papers, vol. 12, Massachusetts Historical Society, Boston.

32. Jonathan Edwards, "Thoughts on the Revival," in *The Works of Jonathan Edwards,* ed. Sereno E. Dwight (New York, 1830), 4:217.

33. For a discussion of Ramist thought and its influence on Puritanism, see Perry Miller, "The Augustinian Strain of Piety," in *The New England Mind: The Seventeenth Century* (New York: Macmillan Co., 1939), chap. 1.

34. Edmund S. Morgan, *The Puritan Family: Religion and Domestic Relations in Seventeenth Century New England* (New York: Harper and Row, 1966), p. 45.

35. Cedric B. Cowing, "Sex and Preaching in the Great Awakening," *American Quarterly* 20 (Fall 1968): 625, finds that in the early eighteenth century women outnumbered men in the churches by a ratio of two to one.

36. Samuel Willard, *A Compleat Body of Divinity* (Boston, 1726), p. 78.

37. Robert Breck, *The Only Methods to Promote the Happiness of the People and Their Posterity* (Boston, 1728), p. 22.

38. John Winthrop, *Journal,* ed. James Kendall Hosner (New York, 1908), 1:317.

39. Quoted in Lawrence Gene Lavengood, "The Great Awakening and New England" (Ph.D. diss., University of Chicago, 1953), pp. 51–52.

40. *The New England Primer: A History of Its Origin and Development, with a Facsimile Reproduction,* ed. Paul Leicester Ford (New York: Dodd, Mead and Co., 1899.

41. Lavengood, *Great Awakening,* p. 39 ff.

42. John Higginson, *The Cause of God and His People in New-England* (Cambridge, 1663), p. 11.

43. Morgan, *Puritan Family,* p. 59.

44. Cotton Mather, *A Family Well-Ordered* (Boston, 1699), p. 3.

45. John Demos, *A Little Commonwealth: Family Life in Plymouth Colony* (New York, 1790), p. 103.

46. Morgan, *Puritan Family,* pp. 47–48.

47. Benjamin Wadsworth, *The Well-Ordered Family* (Boston, 1712), p. 25 ff.

48. A fair amount of attention has been devoted to the question of whether or not women were "better off" in Puritan New England, or in colonial America generally, than they would be in nineteenth-century America. For the sake of clarity, it is best to divide this question into two parts: Did women's lives become more comfortable over time? Did they gain or lose power and prestige over time? The answers to the two questions are not necessarily the same. Nineteenth-century American women, at least middle-class women, clearly led lives that were materially more comfortable than the lives of their seventeenth- and eighteenth-century predecessors had been. On the other hand, it can be argued that nineteenth-century women generally had less power in their families and in society generally, and in an important sense less prestige, than their precedessors had possessed. In Puritan New England,

women's power and prestige were based upon their role in a domestic economy and reinforced by Puritanism, which gave women equal access to sainthood with men and also guaranteed them some social rights.

Recent scholarship suggests that frontier life, not only in New England but in other colonies as well, tended to enhance women's power, even though, at least in Maryland, it also deprived women of some traditional protections. See Lois Green Carr and Lorena Walsh, "The Planter's Wife: The Experience of White Women in Seventeenth-Century Maryland," *William and Mary Quarterly,* 3d ser. 34, no. 4 (October 1977): 542–71. According to Carr and Walsh, the excess of men over women gave women leverage. In New England there was an excess of marriageable men over marriageable women, though not of men over women generally, through the colonial period; see Herbert Moller, "Sex Composition and Correlated Culture Patterns of Colonial America," *William and Mary Quarterly,* 3d ser. 2, no. 2 (April 1945): 113–53. Elisabeth Anthony Dexter, *Colonial Women of Affairs: Women in Business and the Professions in America before 1776* (Boston: Houghton Mifflin, 1931), emphasizes the favorable status of women in colonial America by pointing to the large numbers of women who participated in the economy outside the home. Dexter's view should be qualified, however, by a recognition of the fact that most such women were widows. And Alexander Keyssar, "Widowhood in Eighteenth Century Massachusetts: A Problem in the History of the Family," *Perspectives in American History* 8 (1974): 83–119, shows that such opportunities were unusual even among widows, that most widows faced economic and social hardship.

While a certain level of status and respect was guaranteed to women in colonial America, especially in Puritan New England, the traditional outlook that held sway through the seventeenth and eighteenth centuries also insisted upon women's subordination and inferiority to men. Kenneth Lockridge, *Literacy in Colonial New England: An Enquiry into the Social Context of Literacy in the Early Modern West* (New York: W. W. Norton and Co., 1974), shows that girls were denied access to education beyond the very early years of schooling in most New England towns and that in the eighteenth century women's literacy declined in relation to that of men. Mary Beth Norton, "Eighteenth Century Women in Peace and War: The case of the Loyalists," *William and Mary Quarterly,* 3d ser. 33, no. 3 (July 1976): 386–409, shows that a belief in the inferiority of women to men shaped family relations through the revolutionary period.

A number of historians have suggested that the last decades of the eighteenth century saw an improvement in the position of women: the growth of commerce created new opportunities for women's employment outside the home, and the undermining of traditional attitudes and the spread of an Enlightenment outlook fostered by the Revolution for a time created a space in which women's rights and status could expand. Mary P. Ryan traces this process in her chapter, "Changing Roles, New Risks: Women in Colonial America," in *Womanhood in America: From Colonial Times to the Present* (New York: New Viewpoints, 1975). Nancy F. Cott, "Divorce and the Changing Status of Women in Eighteenth Century Massachusetts," *William and Mary Quarterly,* 3d ser. 33, no. 4 (October 1976): 584–614, shows that in a number of ways women's status in regard to divorce improved in the late eighteenth century. Other historians, concerned primarily with family history rather than the history of women, also show a trend toward more "modern," less "traditional" attitudes: Robert V. Wells, "Quaker Marriage Patterns in a Colonial Perspective," *William and Mary Quarterly,* 3d ser. 29, no. 3 (July 1972): 415–42, and "Family History and Demographic Transition," *Journal of Social History* 9 (Fall 1975): 1–20, shows increasing use of birth control among Quakers; in "Family History," Wells points to and discusses the sources of "modernizing" trends in family relations in this period. Daniel Scott Smith and Michael S. Hindus, "Premarital Pregnancy in America, 1640–1971: An Overview and Interpretation," *Journal of Interdisciplinary History* 5, no. 4 (Spring 1975): 537–70, show an increase in premarital pregnancy in the mid to late eighteenth century, suggesting greater autonomy in decision making on the part of the younger generation. Daniel Scott Smith, "Parental Power and Marriage Patterns: An Analysis of Historical Trends in Hingham, Massachusetts," *Journal of Marriage and the Family* 35 (August 1973): 419–28, argues for the same waning of parental power on the basis of other data. These studies attest to a significant waning of the power of traditional patriarchy in the latter part of the eighteenth century, at least in New England, opening the way for an expansion of the rights of young people and, to some extent, of women.

In the nineteenth century, children and adolescents, at least boys and young men, continued to enjoy greater freedom than had their seventeenth- and early eighteenth-century predecessors; their rights if anything continued to expand. It is the argument of this book that the rights of women were curtailed after this brief period of expansion, that with the hardening of the domestic role and the ideology surrounding it their power and prestige inside the family and out suffered a decline, even though that decline was masked by a sentimental veneration for femininity. This argument corresponds to that put forward by Ryan, *Womanhood in America*; and by Gerda Lerner, "The Lady and the Mill Girl: Changes in the Status of Women in the Age of Jackson," *Midcontinent American Studies Journal* 10 (Spring 1969): 5–15. Daniel Scott Smith, "Family Limitation, Sexual Control, and Domestic Feminism in Victorian America," in *Clio's Consciousness Raised: New Perspectives on the History of Women,* ed. Mary Hartmann and Lois W. Banner (New York: Harper and Row, 1974), pp. 119–36, takes the opposite perspective, stressing the power of female influence within the Victorian family. Nancy F. Cott, *The Bonds of Womanhood: "Woman's Sphere" in New England, 1780–1835* (New Haven: Yale University Press, 1977), takes a position somewhere in between, arguing that within the framework of Victorian domesticity women were accorded certain rights simply by virtue of their femininity but were excluded from areas that some women at least had once been able to enter. Ann Douglas, in *The Feminization of American Culture* (New York: Alfred A. Knopf, 1977), points out that middle-class women in nineteenth-century America had influence. But they thought they had more than they in fact possessed and in any case influence is not the same thing as power.

49. Morgan, *Puritan Family,* p. 58.

50. Leo Kanowitz, *Women and the Law: The Unfinished Revolution* (Albuquerque: University of New Mexico Press, 1969), p. 35 ff. See also Richard B. Morris, "Women's Rights in Early American Law," in *Studies in the History of American Law* (New York: Columbia University Press, 1930), pp. 126–200; and George Haskins, "The Beginnings of Partible Inheritance in the American Colonies," in *Essays in the History of Early American Law ,* ed. David Flaherty (Chapel Hill: Univeristy of North Carolina Press, 1969).

For descriptions of Puritan marriage that emphasize social custom rather than the legal definition of rights, see Chilton H. Powell, "Marriage in Early New England," *New England Quarterly* 1 (July 1928): 323–34; and George E. Howard, *A History of Matrimonial Institutions* (Chicago, 1904), vol. 1.

51. Benjamin Colman, *The Honour and Happiness of the Vertuous Woman* (Boston, 1716), pp. 4–5.

52. Mather, *A Family Well-Ordered,* p. 59.

53. Morgan, *Puritan Family,* pp. 77–78.

54. Cotton Mather, *Ornaments for the Daughters of Zion* (Boston, 1692), pp. 48–49.

55. Thomas Gisborne, *An Enquiry into the Duties of the Female Sex* (London: Caldwell and Davies, 1797), p. 23.

56. Isaac Proctor, Chebacco accounts.

57. John Lendal, ibid.

58. Heaton, "Spiritual Exercises."

59. Bethiah Foster, Chebacco accounts.

60. John Cleaveland, *A Short and Plain Narrative of the Late Work of God's Spirit at Chebacco in Ipswitch in the Years 1763 and 1764* (Boston, 1767), p. 29.

61. Sarah Putridge, Sturbridge accounts.

62. Lucy Allins, ibid.

63. Jemima Harding, ibid.

64. Lucy Proctor, Chebacco accounts.

65. Heaton, "Spiritual Exercises."

66. Jonathan Edwards to Benjamin Colman, May 30, 1735, in *Great Awakening,* ed. Goen, p. 105.

67. Cole, "Born and Born Again."

68. Heaton, "Spiritual Exercises."

69. Cole, "Born and Born Again."

70. Wadsworth, *Well-Ordered Family,* p. 35.

71. Quoted in Morgan, *Puritan Family,* p. 44.

72. Solomon Stoddard, "An Answer to Some Cases of Conscience," quoted in *The Puritans: A Sourcebook of Their Writings,* eds. Perry Miller and Thomas H. Johnson (New York: Harper and Row, 1963), 2:456.

73. Mather, *Ornaments,* p. 59.

74. William Parker to Richard Waldron, November 28, 1741, in Miscellaneous Ms. Letters, Massachusetts Historical Society, Boston.

75. Jonathan Edwards, "Narrative of Surprising Conversions," in *Thoughts on the Revival of Religion in New England, 1740, to Which Is Prefixed a Narrative of the Surprising Work of God in Northampton, Massachusetts, 1735* (Boston, 1740), p. 77.

76. Martha Andrews, Chebacco accounts.

77. Cleaveland, *A Short and Plain Narrative*, p. 29.

78. The assumption that there are fundamental differences between the abilities, and personalities of men and women can be found in a wide array of societies, contemporary and historical, as can the conventional division of labor between men and women, the social basis of differences often presumed to be rooted in biology or natural or religious "law." Feminists have explored the connections between gender-linked personality patterns and the division of labor within the family, according to which women are assigned primary responsibility for child care. See Nancy Chodorow, "Being and Doing: A Cross-Cultural Examination of the Socialization of Males and Females," in *Woman in Sexist Society: Studies in Power and Powerlessness*, ed. Vivian Gornick and Barbara K. Moran (New York: Basic Books, 1971); idem, "Family Structure and Feminine Personality, in *Woman, Culture, and Society*, ed. Michelle Zimbalist Rosaldo and Louise Lamphere (Stanford: Stanford University Press, 1974); idem, *The Reproduction of Mothering: Psychoanalysis and the Sociology of Gender* (Berkeley: University of California Press, 1978); and Dorothy Dinnerstein, *The Mermaid and the Minotaur: Sexual Arrangements and Human Malaise* (New York: Harper and Row, 1976). For discussions of gender and personality less closely linked to the question of mothering, see Michelle Zimbalist Rosaldo, "Woman, Culture, and Society: A Theoretical Overview," and Sherry Ortner, "Is Female to Male as Nature Is to Culture?" both in *Woman, Culture, and Society*, ed. Rosaldo and Lamphere.

CHAPTER TWO

1. Ebenezer Porter, *Letters on the Religious Revivals Which Prevailed about the Beginning of the Present Century* (Boston, 1858), p. 8.

2. Accounts of the Second Great Awakening in New England can be found in the following: Whitney R. Cross, *The Burned-Over District* (Ithaca: Cornell University Press, 1950); Charles Roy Keller, *The Second Great Awakening in Connecticut* (New Haven: Yale University Press, 1942); Timothy L. Smith, *Revivalism and Social Reform: American Protestantism on the Eve of the Civil War* (New York: Abingdon Press, 1957); Bernard A. Weisberger, *They Gathered at the River: The Story of the Great Revivalists and Their Impact upon Religion in America* (Boston: Little, Brown and Co., 1958).

3. *Connecticut Evangelical Magazine and Religious Intelligencer* 1 (1808): 313.

4. Ibid. 7 (1811): 182.

5. Porter, *Letters*, p. 52.

6. William B. Sprague, *Lectures on Revivals of Religion . . . Also an Appendix Consisting of Letters from the Reverend Doctors . . .* (New York, 1833), pp. 40–41.

7. *Connecticut Evangelical Magazine* 1 (1800): 25.

8. Porter, *Letters,* p. 52.

9. Joshua Bradley, *Accounts of Religious Revivals in Many Parts of the United States, from 1815 to 1818* (Albany, 1819), p. 112.

10. Charles Grandison Finney, *Memoirs of Charles G. Finney* (New York, 1876), p. 197.

11. *Connecticut Evangelical Magazine and Religious Intelligencer* 2 (March 1809): 104.

12. *Religious Intelligencer* 2 (1817): 695.

13. *Connecticut Evangelical Magazine* 1 (1800): 62.

14. Ibid. 3 (1803): 63.

15. Ibid., p. 187.

16. Ibid. 1 (1800): 213.

17. *Connecticut Evangelical Magazine and Religious Intelligencer* 7 (1814): 348–49.

18. Hezekiah Harvey, *Memoir of Alfred Bennett, First Pastor of the Baptist Church, Homer, New York* (New York, 1852), p. 125.

19. Melania Smith to Charles G. Finney, Rochester, January 10, 1831, in Papers of Charles G. Finney, Oberlin College Library, Oberlin, Ohio.

20. *Connecticut Evangelical Magazine* 3 (1803): 106.

21. Ibid., p. 102.

22. *Connecticut Evangelical Magazine and Religious Intelligencer* 7 (1816): 461.

23. Melania Smith to Charles G. Finney, Finney Papers.

24. *Connecticut Evangelical Magazine* 3 (1803): 106.

25. William B. Sprague, *Memoir of the Rev. Edward D. Griffin, D.D., Compiled Chiefly from His Own Writings* (New York, 1839), p. 38.

26. *Connecticut Evangelical Magazine* 3 (1803): 109.

27. Orville Dewey, *Letters of an English Traveller to His Friend in England, on the "Revivals of Religion" in America* (Boston, 1828), p. 46.

28. *Religious Intelligencer* 6 (1821): 429.

29. *Connecticut Evangelical Magazine and Religious Intelligencer* 7 (1814): 69.

30. Ibid., p. 233.

31. *Connecticut Evangelical Magazine* 1 (1800): 219.

32. Ibid., p. 61.

33. *Connecticut Evangelical Magazine and Religious Intelligencer* 2 (1809): 69.

34. *Connecticut Evangelical Magazine* 6 (1806): 428.

35. Ibid., p. 429.

36. Ibid. 1 (1800): 33.

37. Ibid. 3 (1803): 107.

38. Presbyterian Church of the U.S.A., Presbytery of Oneida, N.Y., *Narrative of the Revival of Religion in the County of Oneida, in the Year 1826* (Utica, 1826), p. 28.

39. *Connecticut Evangelical Magazine* 1 (1800): 33.

40. Letter of Rev. Edward Griffin, quoted in Sprague, *Lectures on Revivals of Religion,* p. 371.

41. *Rochester* (N.Y.) *Revivalist and Rochester Observer,* October 13, 1832, p. 12.

42. Martin Moore, *Boston Revival, 1842* (Boston, 1842), p. 92.

43. Lyman Beecher, *The Spirit of the Pilgrims* (Boston, 1831–34), 4:563.

44. Jonathan Farr, *These Four Day Meetings* (n.p., n.d., but in pencil, "circa 1831"). Farr is identified as "minister of Gardner, Massachusetts."

45. R. Smith, *Recollections of Nettleton and the Great Revival of 1820* (Albany, 1848), pp. 31–32.

46. Finney, *Memoirs,* p. 197.

47. See Edmund S. Morgan, *The Puritan Family: Religion and Domestic Relations in Seventeenth Century New England* (New York: Harper and Row, 1966), p. 42.

48. See G. J. Barker-Benfield, *The Horrors of the Half-Known Life: Male Attitudes toward Women and Sexuality in Nineteenth Century America* (New York: Harper and Row, 1976).

49. See, for instance, Mrs. Frances Trollope, *Domestic Manners of the Americans* (1832; rpt. ed., New York: Alfred A. Knopf, 1949), p. 117 ff.

50. *Connecticut Evangelical Magazine and Religious Intelligencer* 7 (1814): 238.

CHAPTER THREE

1. The transformation of women's work in early nineteenth-century New England is discussed in Nancy F. Cott, *The Bonds of Womanhood: "Woman's Sphere" in New England, 1780–1835* (New Haven: Yale University Press, 1977). For older descriptions, see Rolla M. Tryon, *Household Manufactures in the United States, 1640–1860* (Chicago: University of Chicago Press, 1917); Alice M. Earle, *Home Life in Colonial Days* (New York: Macmillan Co., 1899).

2. Quoted in Monica Kiefer, *American Children through Their Books, 1700–1835* (Philadelphia; University of Pennsylvania Press, 1948), p. 16.

3. Caleb Bingham, *The American Preceptor* (Troy, N.Y., 1813), pp. 72–73.

4. J. Olney, *The National Preceptor* (Hartford, 1835), p. 162.

5. Amos Jones Cook, *The Student's Companion* (Portland, Me., 1812), p. 127; see also Lindley Murray, *Introduction to the English Reader* (New York, 1809), pp. 43–44; idem, *The English Reader* (New York, 1805), p. 3.

6. Ebenezer Bailey, *The Young Ladies' Class Book* (Boston, 1832), pp. 329–30.

7. Ibid., p. 240.

8. Noah Webster, *An American Selection of Lessons in Reading and Speaking* (Philadelphia, 1787), p. 41.

9. William H. McGuffey, *The Eclectic Fourth Reader* (Cincinnati, 1844), p. 39.

10. John Pierpont, *The American First Class Book*, (Boston, 1835), pp. 329–30.

11. John Pierpont, *The National Reader* (Boston, 1835), p. 20.

12. See Eric Foner, *Free Soil, Free Labor, Free Men: The Ideology of the Republican Party before the Civil War* (New York: Oxford University Press, 1970), p. 11 ff.

13. See Herbert G. Gutman, "The Reality of the Rags-to-Riches 'Myth': The Case of the Paterson, New Jersey, Locomotive, Iron, and Machinery Manufacturers, 1830–1880," in *Work, Culture and Society in Industrializing America: Essays in American Working Class and Social History* (New York: Alfred A. Knopf, 1976), pp. 211–33.

14. Bailey, *Young Ladies' Class Book*, p. 66.

15. Webster, *American Selection of Lessons*, p. 25.

16. Bailey, *Young Ladies' Class Book*, p. 66.

17. Murray, *Introduction*, p. 36.

18. An American Matron, *The Maternal Physician: A Treatise on the Nurture and Management of Infants* (New York, 1811), p. 12.

19. *The Young Lady's Own Book: A Manual of Intellectual Improvement and Moral Deportment* (Philadelphia, 1836), p. 31.

20. *The American Lady's Preceptor: A Compilation of Observations, Essays, and Poetical Effusions, Designed to Direct the Female Mind in a Course of Pleasing and Instructive Reading* (Baltimore, 1813), p. 83.

21. Cott, in a chapter entitled "Domesticity," *Bonds of Womanhood*, traces the development of the rhetoric of domesticity, the language describing men's and women's spheres as separate but equal. In Cott's conclusion, "On 'Women's Sphere' and Feminism," she argues that domesticity was an advance for women in that it provided the basis for a heightening of women's influence within their families and also for a gender-linked consciousness among women that in turn made possible the development of feminism. Cott notes that domesticity had "the defects of its virtues. In opening certain avenues to women because of their sex, it barricaded all others" (p. 201). My disagreement with Cott derives from my view that influence and control are not the same thing and that in a capitalist economy there is a strong link between money and social power. Domesticity enabled men to focus their energies on the task of making money, and the legal structure surrounding domesticity enhanced men's control over family finances. It seems to me that men's and women's "spheres," as they were defined by the nineteenth-century middle class, cannot be regarded as separate or equal and that the inequality of women's position had as much to do with the emergence of feminism as did the female group identity that, as Cott points out, was based on women's common domestic role.

22. John C. Abbott, *The Mother at Home; or, The Principles of Maternal Duty* (Boston, 1833), p. 147.

23. William A. Alcott, *The Young Wife; or, Duties of Woman in the Married Relation* (Boston, 1837), p. 47.

24. Ibid., p. 53.

25. Mrs. Louisa C. Tuthill, *The Young Lady's Home* (Boston, 1847), p. 101.

26. Leo Kanowitz, *Women and the Law: The Unfinished Revolution* (Albuquerque: University of New Mexico Press, 1969), p. 35 ff. See also Isidor Loeb, "Effects of Marriage upon Legal Capacity," *The Legal Property Relations of Married Persons* (New York: Columbia University Press, 1900), pp. 16–48.

27. Heman Humphrey, *Domestic Education* (Amherst, Mass.: J. S. and C. Adams, 1840), p. 16.

28. Mrs. Lydia Child, *The Mother's Book* (Boston, 1831), p. 9.

29. Cotton Mather, *A Family Well-Ordered* (Boston, 1699), p. 10.

30. Abbott, *Mother at Home*; Child, *Mother's Book*.

31. Abbott, *Mother at Home,* p. 159.

32. *The Lady's Companion,* ed. a Lady (Philadelphia, 1856), p. 10.

33. Abbott, *Mother at Home,* p. 159.

34. Margaret Coxe, *The Young Lady's Companion and Token of Affection* (Columbus, Ohio, 1846), p. 11.

35. Alcott, *Young Wife,* p. 69.

36. See Kathryn Kish Sklar, *Catherine Beecher: A Study in American Domesticity* (New Haven: Yale University Press, 1973), pp. 204–16; and Ann Douglas Wood, "The Fashionable Diseases: Women's Complaints and Their Treatment in Nineteenth-Century America," *Journal of Interdisciplinary History* 4, no. 1 (Summer 1973): 25–52.

37. See Helene E. Roberts, "The Exquisite Slave: The Role of Clothes in the Making of the Victorian Woman," *Signs* 2, no. 3 (Spring 1977): 554–69.

38. See Carroll Smith-Rosenberg, "The Hysterical Woman: Sex Roles and Role Conflict in Nineteenth Century America," *Social Research* 39, no. 1 (spring 1972): 652–78.

39. For a fictionalized account of such a treatment and its effect, see Charlotte P. Gilman, *The Yellow Wallpaper* (Boston, 1899; rpt. ed., Old Westbury, N.Y.: Feminist Press, 1973).

CHAPTER FOUR

1. On colonial attitudes toward alcohol and their transformation in the nineteenth century, see Harry Gene Levine, "The Discovery of Addiction: Changing Conceptions of Habitual Drunkenness in American History," paper presented at the meetings of the Society for the Study of Social Problems, New York, August 1976. See also Joseph R. Gusfield, *Symbolic Crusade: Status Politics and the American Temperance Movement* (Urbana: University of Illinois Press, 1963).

2. Cotton Mather, *Sober Considerations on a Growing Flood of Iniquity* (Boston, 1708).

3. W. J. Rorabaugh, "Estimated U.S. Alcoholic Beverage Consumption, 1790–1860," *Journal of Studies on Alcohol* 37, no. 3 (1976): 357–64.

4. Benjamin Rush, *An Inquiry into the Effects of Ardent Spirits upon the Human Body and Mind, with an Account of the Means of Preventing, and of the Remedies for Curing Them,* 7th ed. (Boston: Manning and Loring, 1812).

5. Accounts of the early history of the temperance movement may be found in the following: John A. Krout, *The Origins of Prohibition* (New York: Alfred A. Knopf, 1925); Daniel Dorchester, *The Liquor Problem in All Ages* (New York: Phillips and Hunt, 1884); August Fehlandt, *A Century of Drink Reform in the United States* (Cincinnati: Jennings and Graham, 1904); Ernest H. Cherrington, *The Evolution of Prohibition in the United States of America* (Westerville, Ohio: American Issue Printing Press, 1920); W. H. Daniels, *The Temperance Reform* (New York: Nelson and Philips, 1877).

6. George Packard, M.D., *An Address Delivered before the Female Temperance Society of Saco and Biddeford, June 17, 1838* (Saco, Mass.: S. and C. Webster, 1839).

7. A discussion of the Washington Society can be found in Krout, *Origins of Prohibition,* chap. 9; also, Ian Robert Tyrell, "Drink and the Process of Social Reform: From Temperance to Prohibition in Ante-bellum America, 1813–1860" (Ph.D. diss., Duke University, 1974), chap. 6.

8. My knowledge of the connection between women's temperance and the women's rights movement in this period comes from conversations with Harry Gene Levine and Ellen Du Bois. See in particular Harry Gene Levine, "Temperance and Women in Nineteenth Century United States," in *Research Advances in Alcohol and Drug Problems,* ed. Oriana Kalant et al. (Boston: Wiley, forthcoming), vol. 5.

9. J. H. Beadle, *The Woman's War on Whiskey: Its History, Theory, and Prospects* (Cincinnati: Wilsatch, Baldwin and Co., 1874), p. 5.

10. Jane E. Stebbins, *Fifty Years' History of the Temperance Cause* (Hartford: J. P. Fitch, 1876), pp. 313–14; Mary F. Eastman, *Biography of Dio Lewis* (New York: Fowler and Wells, 1891), p. 66.

11. Quoted in Levine, "Temperance and Women," from Mother Stewart, *Memories of the Crusade: A Thrilling Account of the Great Uprising of the Women of Ohio in 1873 against the Liquor Crime* (Chicago: H. J. Smith, 1890), p. 280.

12. Quoted in Levine, "Temperance and Women," from Mary Earhart, *Frances Willard: From Prayer to Politics* (Chicago: University of Chicago Press, 1944), p. 140.

13. Accounts of the Woman's Crusade may be found in the following: Beadle, *Woman's War on Whiskey*; Mrs. Matilda G. Carpenter, *The Crusade: Its Origin and Development at Washington Court House and Its Results* (Columbus, Ohio: W. C. Hubbard and Co., 1893); Stebbins, *Fifty Years*; Stewart, *Memories of the Crusade*; Annie Wittenmyer, *History of the Woman's Temperance Crusade* (Boston: James H. Earle, c. 1882); Mrs. Eliza Jane Trimble Thompson, Her Two Daughters, and Frances E. Willard, *Hillsboro Crusade Sketches and Family Records* (Cincinnati: Cranston and Curtis, 1896).

14. T. A. Brown, reporter for the *Cincinnati Gazette,* "A Full Description of the Origin and Progress of the New Plan of Labor by the Women up to the Present Time," appended to Stebbins, *Fifty Years,* pp. 326–27.

15. Stebbins, *Fifty Years,* p. 331.

16. Stewart, *Memories of the Crusade,* pp. 150–51.

17. Ibid., p. 153.

18. Carpenter, *The Crusade,* p. 122.

19. Beadle, *Woman's War on Whiskey,* pp. 54–55.

20. Samuel Unger, "A History of the National Woman's Christian Temperance Union" (Ph.D. diss., Ohio State University, 1934), p. 16.

21. Stewart, *Memories of the Crusade,* p. 363.

22. Unger, "History," pp. 18–19.

23. Francis Myron Whitaker, "A History of the Ohio Woman's Christian Temperance Union, 1874–1920" (Ph.D. diss., Ohio State University, 1971), p. 166.

24. Frances E. Willard, *My Happy Half-Century,* ed. Frances E. Cook (London: War, Lock and Bowden, 1894), p. 359.

25. Beadle, *Woman's War on Whiskey,* p. 9.

26. Stewart, *Memories of the Crusade,* pp. 135–36.

27. Ibid., p. 95.

28. Beadle, *Woman's War on Whiskey,* pp. 49–50.

29. Carpenter, *The Crusade,* pp. 43–44.

30. Stewart, *Memories of the Crusade,* pp. 39–40.

31. Ibid., p. 55.

32. Quoted in Levine, "Temperance and Women," from Stewart, *Memories of the Crusade,* pp. 469–70.

33. Quoted in Levine, "Temperance and Women," from John Gough, *Autobiography and Personal Recollections* (Springfield, Mass.: Bill, Nichol, and Co., 1869), p. 185.

34. Stebbins, *Fifty Years,* pp. 244–47.

35. T. S. Arthur, *Ten Nights in a Bar-Room* (Philadelphia: J. W. Bradley, 1854). For the importance of this novel in nineteenth-century popular literature, see Herbert Ross Brown, *The Sentimental Novel in America, 1789–1860* (New York: Pageant Books, 1959), pp. 203–4.

36. Emmet G. Coleman, ed., *The Temperance Songbook* (1907; rpt. ed., New York: American Heritage Press, 1971), pp. 68–69.

37. Rorabaugh, "Estimated alcoholic Beverage Consumption," p. 361.

38. For discussions of temperance and class in early nineteenth-century America, see Alan Dawley, *Class and Community: The Industrial Revolution in Lynn* (Cambridge: Harvard University Press, 1976), pp. 35–37; Paul Faler, "Cultural Aspects of the Industrial Revolution: Lynn, Massachusetts, Shoemakers and Industrial Morality, 1826–1860," *Labor History* 15, no. 3 (Summer 1974): 367–94; and Bruce Laurie, "'Nothing on Impulse': Life Styles of Philadelphia Artisans, 1820–1850," *Labor History* 15, no. 3 (Summer 1974): 337–66. For a dis-

cussion of the role of temperance in the construction of the nineteenth-century American middle class, see Levine, "Temperance and Women."

39. Quoted in Levine, "Temperance and Women," from Samuel Chipman, *The Temperance Lecturer* (1834).

40. Quoted in Unger, "History," p. 25.

41. Thompson et al., *Hillsboro Crusade Sketches*, p. 59.

42. Frances E. Willard, *Woman and Temperance; or, The Work and Workers of the Woman's Christian Temperance Union* (Chicago: Woman's Temperance Publication Association, 1883), p. 78.

43. Dorchester, *Liquor Problem*, pp. 442–43.

44. Stewart, *Memories of the Crusade*, pp. 276–77.

CHAPTER FIVE

1. For a discussion of the social composition of the leadership of the WCTU, see Joseph R. Gusfield, *Symbolic Crusade: Status Politics and the American Temperance Movement* (Urbana: University of Illinois Press, 1963), p. 79 ff. See also Clara C. Chapin, ed., *Thumb Nail Sketches of White Ribbon Women* (Chicago: Woman's Christian Temperance Union, 1895).

2. Norton Mezvinsky, "The White Ribbon Reform, 1874–1920" (Ph.D. diss., University of Wisconsin, 1959), p. 61.

3. Accounts of the early years of the WCTU can be found in Mary Earhart, *Frances Willard: From Prayer to Politics* (Chicago: University of Chicago Press, 1944), chaps. 9, 10; Mezvinsky, "White Ribbon Reform"; and Samuel Unger, "A History of the National Woman's Christian Temperance Union" (Ph.D. diss., Ohio State University, 1934).

4. Earhart, *Frances Willard*, pp. 149 ff.

5. Quoted in Unger, "History," p. 31.

6. An account of the Home Protection ballot campaign can be found in Frances E. Willard, *Woman and Temperance; or, The Work and Workers of the Woman's Christian Temperance Union* (Chicago: Woman's Temperance Publication Association, 1883), p. 450 ff.

7. Quoted in Earhart, *Frances Willard*, p. 161.

8. My statistics are drawn from Norton Mezvinsky, "White-Ribbon Reform," pp. 68 ff.

9. Earhart, *Frances Willard*, p. 184.

10. "Annual Minutes of the National Woman's Christian Temperance Union" (WCTU Library, Evanston, Ill.), 21st meeting, 1894, p. 106.

11. Quoted in Willard, *Woman and Temperance*, chap. 14.

12. Earhart, *Frances Willard*, p. 197.

13. Ibid., p. 212 ff.

14. See, for instance, a letter from Catharine P. Wallace, *Union Signal*, May 3, 1888, p. 5.

15. Earhart, *Frances Willard*, p. 238 ff.

16. "Annual Minutes," 21st meeting, 1894, p. 106.

17. Ibid., 12th meeting, 1885, p. 73.

18. Ibid., 21st meeting, 1894, p. 85.

19. Ibid., 15th meeting, 1888, p. 25.

20. *Union Signal,* December 3, 1885, pp. 4–5.

21. Anna Garlin Spencer, *Union Signal,* December 9, 1886, p. 5.

22. Unger, "History," p. 228.

23. Frances E. Willard, *A White Life for Two,* Gospel Purity Series (Chicago: Woman's Christian Temperance Union, 1890), p. 3.

24. George M. Jobson, *Manual of the White Shield Society* (Richmond, Va.: Woman's Christian Temperance Union, n.d.), p. 2.

25. *Union Signal,* January 14, 1887, p. 12.

26. "Annual Minutes," 15th meeting, 1888, p. 122.

27. Unger, "History," p. 229.

28. *Union Signal,* November 28, 1889, p. 3.

29. "Annual Minutes," 19th meeting, 1892, p. 113.

30. Mary Livermore, *Union Signal,* March 8, 1883, p. 2.

31. *Union Signal,* September 10, 1891, pp. 4–5.

32. Ibid., January 28, 1892, p. 2.

33. Ibid., September 10, 1891, p. 4.

34. "Annual Minutes," 19th meeting, 1892, p. 94.

35. Rachel Foster Avery, *Union Signal,* January 24, 1895, p. 4.

36. Anna Carpenter, ibid., April 4, 1895, p. 4.

37. Rachel Foster Avery, *ibid.,* April 25, 1895, p. 5.

38. Jennie Logue Campbell, *ibid.,* May 9, 1895, p. 4.

39. Ibid., May 16, 1895, p. 2.

40. Ibid., November 18, 1886, p. 2.

41. Ibid., October 31, 1895, p. 9.

42. Ibid., May 2, 1889, p. 2.

43. Ibid., August 22, 1889, p. 3.

44. "Annual Minutes," 21st meeting, 1894, p. 85.

45. *Union Signal,* March 8, 1888, p. 2.

46. Ibid., November 8, 1883.

47. Frances E. Willard, *Glimpses of Fifty Years: The Autobiography of an American Woman* (Chicago, 1889), p. 465 ff.

48. "Annual Minutes," 22d annual meeting, 1895, p. 59.

49. For a discussion of the Knights of Labor and of the political and social outlook of its leadership, see Norman Ware, *The Labor Movement in the United States, 1860–1895* (New York: D. Appleton and Co., 1929), pp. 22–242.

50. Willard, *Glimpses of Fifty Years,* p. 423; Earhart, *Frances Willard,* p. 248.

51. *Union Signal,* April 1, 1886, p. 5.

52. Ella A. Boole, ibid., February 14, 1895, p. 2.

53. "Annual Minutes," 19th meeting, 1892, p. 129.

54. Ibid., 22d meeting, 1895, p. 60.

55. Ibid., 19th meeting, 1892, p. 130.

56. For a discussion of Frances Willard's socialism, see Earhart, *Frances Willard,* chap. 18. For Willard's own statement, see "Gospel Socialism," pp. 104–12 of her address in "Annual Minutes," 20th meeting, 1893.

57. Earhart, *Frances Willard,* p. 290.

58. "Annual Minutes," 20th meeting, 1893, p. 106.

59. Ibid., p. 105.

60. Ibid., 21st meeting, 1894, p. 120.

61. *Union Signal,* February 7, 1895, pp. 8–9.

62. Ibid., January 24, 1895, p. 7.

63. Earhart, *Frances Willard,* p. 360.

64. "Annual Minutes," 22d annual meeting, 1895, p. 105.

65. Mezvinsky, "White Ribbon Reform," p. 248 ff., and Francis Myron Whitaker, "A History of the Ohio Woman's Christian Temperance Union" (Ph.D. diss., Ohio State University, 1971), pp. 386 ff., 443 ff.

66. James H. Timberlake, *Prohibition and the Progressive Movement, 1900–1920* (Cambridge: Harvard University Press, 1963), pp. 153 ff., and Whitaker, "History," p. 447 ff.

Sources

ACCOUNTS OF RELIGIOUS REVIVALS AND CONVERSIONS

Baldwin, Dr., Pastor of the Second Baptist Church in Boston. *A Brief Sketch of the Revival of Religion in Boston, in 1803–5.* Boston, 1804.

Baldwin, Thomas. *A Brief Account of the Late Revivals of Religion in a Number of Towns in the New-England States.* Boston, 1799.

Baptist Religious Society. Papers. Old Sturbridge Village Library, Sturbridge, Mass.

Beecher, Rev. Dr. Lyman, and Nettleton, Asahel. *Letters of the Rev. Dr. Nettleton, on the "New Measures" in Conducting Revivals of Religion.* New York, 1828.

Bellamy, Joseph. Letters. Archives, Case Memorial Library, Hartford Theological Seminary, Hartford, Conn.

———. Papers. Connecticut Historical Society, Hartford.

Bradley, Joshua. *Accounts of Religious Revivals in Many Parts of the United States, from 1815 to 1818.* Albany, 1819.

Brockway, J. *A Delineation of the Characteristic Features of the Revival of Religion in Troy, in 1826 and 1827.* Troy, N.Y., 1827.

Buel, Samuel. *A Faithful Narrative of the Remarkable Revival of Religion in the Congregation of Easthampton on Long-Island, in the Year of Our Lord, 1764 . . . And, Also, an Account of the Revival of Religion in Bridgehampton and Easthampton, in the Year 1800.* Sag Harbor, N.Y., 1808.

Caldwell, John. *A Sermon Preached at New Londonderry, Oct. 14, 1741: An Impartial Trial of the Spirit Operating in This Part of the World.* Boston, 1742.

Chauncy, Charles. *Seasonable Thoughts on the State of Religion in New England.* Boston, 1743.

Cleaveland, John. Papers. Essex Institute Historical Library, Salem, Mass.

———. *A Short and Plain Narrative of the Late Work of God's Spirit at Chebacco in Ipswitch in the Years 1763 and 1764.* Boston, 1767.

Cole, Nathan. Ms. vol. "Born 1711 and Born Again 1741." Connecticut Historical Society, Hartford.

Colman, Benjamin. Papers. Massachusetts Historical Society, Boston.

Congregationalist Church of the United States, Oneida Association, N.Y. *Pastoral Letter of the Ministers of the Oneida Association to the Churches under Their Care, on the Subject of Revivals of Religion.* Utica, 1827.

Cushman, Rev. R. W. *A Calm Review of the Measures Employed in the Religious Awakening in Boston, in 1742.* Boston, 1846.

Dewey, Orville. *Letters of an English Traveller to His Friend in England, on the "Revivals of Religion" in America.* Boston, 1828.

Douglas, James. *The Revival of Religion: To Which Is Added, An Account of the Revival at Kilsyth, by Rev. Burns.* Edinburgh, 1839.

Duncan, Mary (Grey) Lundie. *History of Revivals of Religion in the British Isles, Especially in Scotland.* Edinburgh, 1836.

Dwight, Timothy. *A Discourse in Two Parts.* New Haven, 1812.

Eastman, C. G. *Sermons, Addresses, and Exhortations, by Jedediah Burchard, with an Appendix, containing some account of proceedings during protracted meetings, held under his direction in Burlington, Williston, and Hinesburgh, Vermont, December, 1835 and January, 1836.* Burlington, 1836.

Edwards, Jonathan. Papers. Beinecke Rare Book Library, Yale University, New Haven, Conn.

———. *Thoughts on the Revival of Religion in New England, 1740, to Which Is Prefixed a Narrative of the Surprising Work of God in Northampton, Massachusetts, 1735.* Boston, 1740.

Farr, Jonathan. *On Revivals.* Boston, 1831.

———, Minister of Gardner, Mass. *These Four Day Meetings.* N.p., n.d.; "circa 1831."

Finney, Charles G. *Memoirs.* New York, 1876.

———. Papers. Oberlin College Library, Oberlin, Ohio.

Gammage, Smith P. *Fact Not Fiction; or, The Remarkable History of Mrs. Louisa Liscum.* New York, 1840.

Gannett, Ezra Stiles. *A Comparison of the Good and the Evil of Revivals.* Boston, 1831.

Griffin, Edward D. *A Letter to the Rev. Ansel D. Eddy, of Canandaigua, N.Y., on the Narrative of the Late Revivals of Religion, in the Presbytery of Geneva.* Williamstown, Mass., 1832.

Hall, Rev. James. *Narrative of a Most Extraordinary Work of Religion in North Carolina: To Which Is Added, Intelligence of a Revival in South Carolina, and in Washington County, Pennsylvania.* Philadelphia, 1803.

Harvey, Hezekiah. *Memoir of Alfred Bennett, First Pastor of the Baptist Church, Homer, New York.* New York, 1852.

Hauses, J. *Reminiscences of Revivals of Religion in the First Church in Hartford.* Hartford, Conn., 1865.

Heaton, Hannah Cook. "Experiences or Spiritual Exercises." Ms. diary. Connecticut Historical Society, Hartford.

Hopkins, Samuel. *Memoir of the Life of Mrs. Sarah Osborn who died at Newport (Rhode-Island) on the second day of August, 1796, in the 83rd year of her age.* Catskill, N.Y., 1814.

Humphrey, Rev. Heman. *Revival Sketches and Manual.* New York, 1859.

Jennings, Rev. E., of Dalton, Mass. *A Portrait of What Are Called the "New Measures" as They Appeared in the County of Berkshire (Mass.) in the Years 1833-4: By an Eye-Witness.* Troy, N.Y., 1835.

Keep, John. *A Narrative of the Origin and Progress of the Congregational Church in Homer, Cortland County, New York . . . (By J. K., Pastor of the Church.)* Homer, 1833.

———. *Review of a Narrative.* Syracuse, N.Y., 1833.

A Letter from an Eminent Minister in the Church of Scotland: written to a Minister of his Acquaintance at some distance in the same Kingdom. Boston, 1773.

A Letter from a Gentleman in Boston, to Mr. George Wishart, One of the Ministers of Edinburgh, Concerning the State of Religion in New England. Edinburgh, 1742.

McCulloch, Rev. William. "Examination of Persons under Spiritual Concern at Cambusland, during the Revival, in 1741-42, with Marginal Notes by Dr. Webster and Other Ministers." 2 volumes. MS. New College Library, Edinburgh.

MacFarlan, D. *The Revivals of the Eighteenth Century, Particularly at Cambuslang.* Edinburgh, n.d.

McGavin, William. *Letters on the State of Religion in Some Parts of the Highlands of Scotland.* Glasgow, 1818.

MacGillivray, Rev. Angus. *Sketches of Religion and Revivals of Religion in the North Highlands during the Last Century.* Edinburgh, 1849.

Martyn, J. M., Pastor of Said Church. *A Narrative of the Origin and Progress of the First Free Congregational Church, in Buffalo, New York: With an Account of Their Late Protracted Meeting.* Buffalo, 1834.

Merrill, Abel K. Letters to his fianceé, Mary Leverell, re a revival in Haverhill, N.H., 1830. Ms. Congregational Library, Boston.

Moore, Martin. *Boston Revival, 1842.* Boston, 1842.

Morton, Daniel O., Pastor of the Congregational Church in Springfield, Vt. *A Narrative of a Revival of Religion in Springfield, Vermont.* Springfield, 1834.

A Narrative of the Surprising Work of God in the Conversion of Souls in Kilsyth, Finneidston, and Cumbernault; and the Revival of Religion in Anderston and Paisley; with an account of the remarkable occurrances . . . at Kilsyth, on 22 September, 1838. Glasgow, 1839.

Nettleton, Asahel. Letters. Archives, Case Memorial Library, Hartford Theological Seminary. Hartford, Conn.

———. *Rev. Asahel Nettleton's Letter to Dr. Lyman Beecher, on Revivals.* N.p., n.d.; in pencil, "circa 1831."

Osborne, Mrs. Sarah. *The Nature, Certainty, and Evidence of True Christianity, in a Letter from a Gentlewoman, in Rhode-Island, to Another, Her Dear Friend, in Great Darkness, Doubt, and Concern, of a Religious Nature.* Providence, 1743.

Perkins, Ephraim. *A "Bunker Hill" Contest,* AD *1826, between the "holy alliance" for the establishment of hierarchy and ecclesiastical domination over the human mind, on the one side, and the asserters of free inquiry, bible religion, christian freedom, and civil liberty on the other.* Utica, N.Y., 1826.

Perkins, Nathan. *Two Discourses on the Grounds of the Christian's Hope: Containing a Brief Account of the Work of God's Holy Spirit, in a Remarkable Revival of Religion in West-Hartford, in This Year 1799.* Hartford, Conn., 1800.

Porter, E. *Letters on the Religious Revivals Which Prevailed about the Beginning of the Present Century.* Boston, 1858.

Presbyterian Church of the U.S.A., Presbytery of Albany, N.Y. *A Narrative of the Revival of Religion, within the Bounds of the Presbytery of Albany, in the Year 1820.* Schenectady, N.Y., 1821.

———, Presbytery of Geneva, N.Y. *A Narrative of the Late Revivals of Religion, within the Bounds of Geneva Presbytery.* Geneva, 1832.

———, Presbytery of Oneida, N.Y. *Narrative of the Revival of Religion in the County of Oneida, in the Year 1826.* Utica, N.Y., 1826.

Prince, Thomas. *An Account of the Great Revival in Middleborough, Massachusetts,* A.D. *1741, 1742.* Rpt.; Boston, 1842.

———. *An Account of the Revival of Religion in Boston, in the Years 1740–3.* Rpt.; Boston, 1823.

———, ed. *The Christian History.* Boston, 1743–44.

Rayner, Rev. Menzies. *A Dissertation upon Extraordinary Awakenings, or Religious Stirs; Conversion, Regeneration, Renovation, and a Change of Heart; Conference Meetings; Extraordinary Gifts in Extempore Prayer; Evangelical Preaching; etc.* New Haven, 1816.

Robe, James. *Narrative of the Revival of Religion at Kilsyth. Cambuslang, and Other Places, in 1742.* Glasgow, 1840.

―――. *Narratives of the Extraordinary Work of the Spirit of God at Cambuslang, Kilsyth, etc., Begun 1742.* Glasgow, 1840.

Roots, Peter Philanthropos. *A Letter to the First Congregational Paedobaptist Church, at Rutland in Vermont . . . Also Dr. Robbins' Account of a Late Revival of Religion at Plymouth, in Massachusetts.* Hartford, 1794.

A Short Account of the Remarkable Conversions at Cambuslang: In a Letter from a Gentleman in the West-Country to His Friend at Edinburgh. Glasgow, 1742.

Skinner, Otis Ainsworth. *Letters to Rev. B. Stow, R. H. Neale, and R. W. Cushman, on Modern Revivals.* Boston, 1842.

Smith, Rev. R. *Recollections of Nettleton and the Great Revival of 1820.* Albany, 1848.

Sprague, William B. *Lectures on Revivals of Religion . . . Also an appendix consisting of letters from the Reverend Doctors . . .* New York, 1833.

―――, Minister of the Second Presbyterian Church in Albany. *Memoir of the Rev. Edward D. Griffin, D.D., Compiled Chiefly from his own Writings.* New York, 1839.

Stewart, Alexander. *Account of a Late Revival of Religion in a Part of the Highlands of Scotland.* Edinburgh, 1800.

Streeter, Russell. *Mirror of Calvinistic Fanaticism; or, Jedediah Burchard and Company.* Woodstock, Vt., 1835.

The Testimony and Advice of an Assembly of Pastors of Churches in New-England, at a Meeting in Boston, July 7, 1743, Occasioned by the late happy Revival of Religion in many parts of the land. Boston, 1743.

Times of Refreshing: Being Notices of Some of the Religious Awakenings which have taken place in the U.K., with special Reference to the Revival in Aberdeen. Aberdeen, 1859.

Tyler, Bennett. *New England Revivals as They Existed at the Close of the Eighteenth and the Beginning of the Nineteenth Centuries.* Boston, 1846.

Wadsworth, Daniel. Ms. diary, 1728–46. Connecticut Historical Society, Hartford.

Walton, W. C., Pastor of Said Church. *Narrative of a Revival of Religion in the Third Presbyterian Church in Baltimore.* Northhampton, Mass., 1826.

Weeks, William R. *A Letter of Protracted Meetings, Addressed to the Church in Paris.* Utica, N.Y., 1832.

Whitman, Bernard. *Letter to an Orthodox Minister on Revivals of Religion.* Boston, 1831.

Wishart, George. *The Case of Offences against Christianity Considered.* Edinburgh, 1742.

Woodward, W. W. *Increase of Piety; or, The Revival of Religion in the United States of America.* Philadelphia, 1801.

RELIGIOUS PERIODICALS

Connecticut Evangelical Magazine. Hartford.

New York Evangelist and Religious Review. New York.

Religious Intelligencer. Hartford.

Rochester Revivalist and Rochester Observer. Rochester, N.Y.

PURITAN TRACTS ON WOMEN AND THE FAMILY

Colman, Benjamin. *The Honour and Happiness of the Vertuous Woman.* Boston, 1716.

Mather, Cotton. *A Family Well-Ordered.* Boston, 1699.

———. *Ornaments for the Daughters of Zion.* Boston, 1692.

Wadsworth, Benjamin. *The Well-Ordered Family.* Boston, 1712.

GUIDEBOOKS FOR WOMEN AND A FEW FOR YOUNG MEN

Abbott, John C., Pastor of the Calvinist Church, Worcester, Mass. *The Mother at Home; or, The Principles of Maternal Duty.* Boston, 1833.

Alcott, William A. *The Young Mother; or, Management of Children in Regard to Health.* Boston, 1838.

———. *The Young Wife; or, Duties of Woman in the Married Relation.* Boston, 1837.

———. *The Young Woman's Guide.* 1836; rpt., New York, 1852.

The American Lady's Preceptor: A Compilation of Observations, Essays, and Poetical Effusions, Designed to Direct the Female Mind in a Course of Pleasing and Instructive Reading. Baltimore, 1813.

Bennett, John. *Strictures on Female Education.* Worcester, Mass., 1795.

Burton, J. *Lectures on Female Education and Manners.* London, 1793.

Carey, M. *Philosophy of Common Sense: Practical Rules for the Promotion of Domestic Happiness.* Philadelphia, 1837.

Child, Mrs. Lydia. *The Mother's Book.* Boston, 1831.

Coxe, Margaret. *The Young Lady's Companion and Token of Affection.* Columbus, Ohio, 1846.

Eddy, Rev. Daniel C. *Lectures to Young Ladies on Subjects of Practical Importance.* Lowell, Mass., 1848.

Ellis, Mrs. Sarah. *Family Secrets; or, Hints to Those Who Would Make Home Happy.* 3 vols. London, 1841.

The Family Book; or, Instructions Concerning All the Relations of Life. New York, 1835.

Farrar, Mrs. Eliza [A Lady]. *The Young Lady's Friend.* Boston, 1837.

Gisborne, Thomas. *An Enquiry into the Duties of the Female Sex.* London: Caldwell and Davies, 1797.

Hoare, Louisa. *Hints for the Improvement of Early Education and Nursery Discipline.* Salem, Mass., 1827.

Humphrey, Heman, President of Amherst College. *Domestic Education.* Amherst, Mass.: J. S. and C. Adams, 1840.

Kendal, David. *The Young Lady's Arithmetic.* Leominster, Mass., 1797.

The Lady's Companion. Edited by a Lady. Philadelphia, 1856.

The Lady's Pocket Companion and Indispensable Friend. New York, 1858.

The Maternal Physician: A Treatise on the Nurture and Management of Infants. By an American Matron. New York, 1811.

The Mother's Friend; or, Familial Directions for Forming the Mental and Moral Habits of Young Children. New York, 1834.

My Daughter's Manual, Comprising a Summary View of Female Studies, Accomplishments, and Principles of Conduct. New York, 1838.

Pennington, Sarah. *An Unfortunate Mother's Advice to Her Absent Daughter: In a letter to Miss Pennington.* London, 1761.

Pilkington, Mrs. *Historical Beauties for Young Ladies. Intended to lead the Female Mind to the Love and Practice of Moral Goodness. Designed principally for the Use of Ladies' Schools.* London, 1798.

Rush, Benjamin. "Thoughts upon Female Education, Accommodated to the Present State of Society, Manners, and Government in the United States of America" (Boston, 1787). In Frederich Rudolph, ed., *Essays on Education in the Early Republic.* Cambridge, Mass., 1965.

Sigourney, Mrs. L. H. *The Young Ladies' Offering; or, Gems of Prose and Poetry.* Boston, 1849.

Sprague, William B. *Letters on Practical Subjects to a Daughter.* New York, n.d.

Taylor, Isaac. *Home Education.* New York, 1838.

Thornwell, Emily. *The Lady's Guide to Perfect Gentility.* New York, 1856.

Thoughts on Domestic Education, the Result of Experience, by a Mother. Boston, 1829.

Tuthill, Mrs. Louisa C. *The Belle, the Blue, and the Bigot; or, Three Fields for Woman's Influence.* Providence, 1844.

————. *I Will Be a Gentleman: A Book for Boys.* Boston, 1852.

————. *My Wife.* Boston, 1846.

————. *The Young Lady's Home.* Boston, 1847.

West, Mrs. *Letters to a Young Lady.* London, 1806.

The Wife, and Woman's Reward. 2 vols. New York, 1835.

Winslow, Rev. Hubbard, and Sanford, Mrs. John. *The Lady's Manual of Moral and Intellectual Culture.* New York, 1854. Published earlier as *Woman as She Should Be.*

The Young Ladies' Friend. By a Lady. Boston, 1837.

The Young Lady's Gift. Providence, n.d.

The Young Lady's Guide. New York, 1870.

The Young Lady's Mentor. By a Lady. Philadelphia, 1858.

The Young Lady's Own Book: A Manual of Intellectual Improvement and Moral Deportment. Philadelphia, 1836.

The Young Lady's Sunday Book. Philadelphia, 1834.

The Young Woman's Monitor: Shewing the Great Happiness of Early Piety, and the Dreadful Consequences of Forsaking the Path of Virtue. London, 1787.

SCHOOLBOOKS

Bailey, Ebenezer. *The Young Ladies' Class Book.* Boston, 1832.

Bingham, Caleb. *The American Preceptor.* "Seventh Troy Edition"; Troy, N.Y., 1813.

Cook, Amos Jones, Preceptor of Freeburg Academy. *The Student's Companion.* Portland, Me., 1812.

Cotton, John. *Spiritual Milk for Boston Babes.* Cambridge, Mass., 1656.

Emerson, Benjamin Dudley. *Third-Class Reader.* N.p., n.d.

Frost, John. *The Class Book of American Literature.* Boston, 1826.

Goodrich, S. G. *The Fourth Reader.* Louisville, Ky., 1839.

Harrod, John J. *The Academical Reader.* Baltimore, 1832.

McGuffey, William H. *The Eclectic Fourth Reader.* Cincinnati, 1844.

————. *McGuffey's Newly Revised Fourth Reader.* Cincinnati, 1844.

————. *McGuffey's Rhetorical Guide; or, Fifth Reader of the Eclectic Series.* New York, 1843.

Murray, Lindley. *English Grammar.* 1795; rpt., Menston, England, 1968.

————. *English Grammar.* Vols. 1, 2. New York, 1809.

————. *The English Reader.* New York, 1805.

————. *Introduction to the English Reader.* New York, 1809.

Olney, J. *The National Preceptor*. Hartford, 1835.

Pierpont, John. *The American First Class Book*. Boston, 1835.

Webster, Noah. *An American Selection of Lessons in Reading and Speaking*. Philadelphia, 1787.

TEMPERANCE: HISTORIES, MEMOIRS, CONTEMPORARY ACCOUNTS, PUBLICATIONS

"Annual Minutes of the National Woman's Christian Temperance Union." Library of the Woman's Christian Temperance Union, Evanston, Ill.

Arthur, T. S. *Ten Nights in a Bar-Room*. Philadelphia: J. W. Bradley, 1854; rpt., New York, 1966.

Beadle, J. H. *The Woman's War on Whiskey: Its History, Theory, and Prospects*. Cincinnati: Wilsatch, Baldwin and Co., 1874.

Beattie, Donald Weldon. "Sons of Temperance: Pioneers in Total Abstinence and 'Constitutional' Prohibition." Ph.D. diss., Boston University, 1966.

Carpenter, Mrs. Matilda Gilruth. *The Crusade: Its Origin and Development at Washington Court House and Its Results*. Columbus, Ohio: W. C. Hubbard and Co., 1893.

Chapin, Clara C., ed. *Thumb Nail Sketches of White Ribbon Women*. Chicago: Woman's Christian Temperance Union, 1895.

Cherrington, Ernest H. *The Evolution of Prohibition in the United States of America*. Westerville, Ohio: American Issue Printing Press, 1920.

Coleman, Emmet C., ed. *The Temperance Songbook*. 1907; rpt., New York; American Heritage Press, 1971.

Daniels, W. H. *The Temperance Reform*. New York: Nelson and Philips, 1877.

Dorchester, Daniel. *The Liquor Problem in All Ages*. New York: Phillips and Hunt, 1884.

Earhart, Mary. *Frances Willard: From Prayer to Politics*. Chicago, University of Chicago Press, 1944.

Eastman, Mary F. *Biography of Dio Lewis*. New York: Fowler and Wells, 1891.

Fehlandt, August. *A Century of Drink Reform in the United States*. Cincinnati: Jennings and Graham, 1904.

Gordon, Anna A. *The Beautiful Life of Frances Willard*. Evanston, Ill.: The Union Signal, 1898.

————, ed. *What Frances E. Willard Said*. Chicago: F. H. Revell, 1905.

Gordon, Elizabeth Putnam. *Women Torch-Bearers*. Evanston, Ill.: NWCTU Publishing House, 1924.

Gusfield, Joseph R. *Symbolic Crusade: Status Politics and the American Temperance Movement.* Urbana: University of Illinois Press, 1963.

Hoover, Charles. *Intemperance in Relation to Family Interests and Happiness.* National Division of the Sons of Temperance, 1849.

Jobson, George M. *Manual of the White Shield Society.* Richmond, Va.: Woman's Christian Temperance Union, n.d.

Krout, John A. *The Origins of Prohibition.* New York: Alfred A. Knopf, 1925.

Levine, Harry Gene. "The Discovery of Addiction: Changing Conceptions of Habitual Drunkenness in American History." Paper presented at the meetings of the Society for the Study of Social Problems, New York, August 1976.

———. "Temperance and Women in Nineteenth Century United States." In *Research Advances in Alcohol and Drug Problems,* vol. 5. Edited by Oriana Kalant et al. Boston: Wiley, forthcoming.

Mezvinsky, Norton. "The White Ribbon Reform, 1874–1920." Ph.D. diss., University of Wisconsin, 1959.

Packard, George, M.D. *An Address Delivered before the Female Temperance Society of Saco and Biddeford, June 17, 1838.* Saco, Mass.: S. and C. Webster, 1839.

Rush, Benjamin. *An Inquiry into the Effects of Ardent Spirits upon the Human Body and Mind, with an Account of the Means of Preventing, and of the Remedies for Curing Them.* 7th ed. Boston: Manning and Loring, 1812.

Stebbins, Jane E. *Fifty Years, History of the Temperance Cause.* Hartford: J. P. Fitch, 1876.

Stewart, Eliza A. [Mother]. *Memories of the Crusade.* Chicago: H. J. Smith, 1890.

Thompson, Mrs. Eliza Jane Trimble; Her Two Daughters; and Willard, Frances E. *Hillsboro Crusade Sketches and Family Records.* Cincinnati: Cranston and Curtis, 1896.

Timberlake, James H. *Prohibition and the Progressive Movement, 1900–1920.* Cambridge: Harvard University Press, 1963.

Turner, James Ross. "The American Prohibition Movement, 1865–1897." Ph.D. diss., University of Wisconsin, 1972.

Tyrell, Ian Robert. "Drink and the Process of Social Reform: From Temperance to Prohibition in Ante-bellum America, 1813–1860." Ph.D. diss., Duke University, 1974.

Unger, Samuel. "A History of the National Woman's Christian Temperance Union." Ph.D. diss., Ohio State University, 1934.

Union Signal. Chicago.

Whitaker, Francis Myron. "A History of the Ohio Woman's Christian Temperance Union, 1874–1920." Ph.D. diss., Ohio State University, 1971.

Willard, Frances E. *Do Everything: A Handbook for the World's White Ribboners.* Chicago, 1895.

———. *Glimpses of Fifty Years: The Autobiography of an American Woman.* Chicago, 1889.

———. *History of the National Woman's Christian Temperance Union.* New York, 1876.

———. *Home Protection Manual: Containing an Argument for the Temperance Ballot for Woman, and How to Obtain It, as a Means of Home Protection; also Constitution and Plan of Work for State and Local W.C.T. Unions.* New York, 1879.

———. *My Happy Half-Century.* Edited by Frances E. Cook. London: War, Lock and Bowden, 1894.

———. *A White Life for Two.* Chicago: Woman's Christian Temperance Union, 1890.

———. *Women and Temperance; or, The Work and Workers of the Woman's Christian Temperance Union.* Chicago: Woman's Temperance Publication Association, 1883.

Wittenmyer, Annie. *History of the Woman's Temperance Crusade.* Boston: James H. Earle, c. 1882.

Index

"Sabbath reform," 139, 141
Salvation, 47, 48, 53, 73; in Puritan society, 21, 23–24, 34
Schools. *See* Education, public
Second Great Awakening of 1797–1840, 45–65; antagonism between the sexes and, 48, 59–64, 65, 87; church as center of women's reforms during, 1, 64, 65, 87; conversion themes, 47, 51, 53–62; converts during, 45–52, 67; female converts during, 55–62, 65, 87; male converts during, 52–55, 73; men's resistance to Calvinism, 48–52, 73; ministry and, 45–48, 56–57, 61; secular concerns of women during, 1. *See also* Domesticity; Great Awakening of 1740–44
Secularism, 13; liberty as ideal of, 68–73; public education and, 67–73
Sermons, 30; conversion experiences after, 15, 16, 18
Sexual fantasies and conversion experience, 40
Sexuality, 136; linked with women by Puritans, 42–43; nineteenth-century woman and double standard, 86, 126–27; "the white life," 126–28, 148
Sexes, reorganization of relationship between, 4, 8, 9. *See also* Labor, division of
Shaw, Anna, 121
Shaw, Rev. Anna Howard, 133
Shaw, Eleanor E., 133
Shumway, Mary, 20–21
Sin and conversion, 15, 16–17, 37, 38, 40, 47, 48, 51, 55, 57. *See also* Original sin
Slavery, 73, 74
Smith, Raymond W., 133
Socialism, 137, 142–44
Socialist party, 143
Social mobility, 3, 69, 72, 104
Society for the Suppression of Vice, 129
Society for the White Cross, 127
Somerset, Lady, 142, 144, 145
Sons of Temperance, The, 93
Southwestern Railroad strike of 1886, 138
Stanton, Elizabeth Cady, 93
Stevens, Mrs. L. M. N., 135
Stewart, Mother, 94, 103–4
Stockbridge, Massachusetts, 56–57
Stoddard, Solomon, 42

Sturbridge, Massachusetts, conversion accounts from, 6, 16, 19, 20, 39
Suffrage for women, 2, 4, 116, 118–20, 123, 124–25, 129–30, 132, 147, 148; "Home Protection" ballot, 118–19, 120, 121, 148; Knights of Labor and, 139
Suicide, contemplation of, 15, 20, 53, 58

Taylor, Edward, 90–91
Temperance movement, 1, 3, 4, 5, 9, 89–146; literature of, 105–7; origins of, 91–95, 108; sources of the women's movement, 107–14; women's role in origins, 89, 92, 93–94. *See also* Woman's Christian Temperance Union; Woman's Crusade of 1873–75
Ten Nights in a Bar-Room (Arthur), 105
Thompson, Mrs. Eliza, 111–12
Torrington, Connecticut, 58
Towns, growth of: change in women's roles and, 2, 3, 7, 65, 78–79; the upper-class lady and, 35–40; Second Great Awakening and, 45, 46; Woman's Christian Temperance Union and, 116
Trade unions, 137, 138
Tuthill, Louisa, 78–79

Union Signal, 7, 119, 123, 126, 127, 129, 130–31, 133–36, 139–40, 143–44
Unitarianism, 49, 50; ministers, 8
Universalism, 49, 50; ministers, 8
Urbanization. *See* Towns, growth of

Van Pelt, Charles, 96–97
Venereal disease, 86, 148
Victorian morality, 125–28, 133, 146, 148, 149
Visions, 15

Wadsworth, Benjamin, 30, 41
Washington Court House, Ohio, 95
Washington Society, 92–93
Wealth: Puritan view of, 24; secular view of, 68–69, 71–72
Well-Ordered Family, The (Wadsworth), 30
West Simsbury, Connecticut, 57
Wheeling, West Virginia, 112–13
Whitefield, George, 12, 16
"White life, the," 126–28, 148